COPYRIGHT

D1627956

Edited by Sam Winsbury

Cover design by Blab

Typesetting by Blab

Typeset in Rift & Museo Sans

Published by UK Book Publishing
www.ukbookpublishing.com

ISBN: 978-1-914195-84-6

HOW TO MAKE YOUR AGENCY WORK FOR YOU

FOREWORD

When I met Jonathan I was sceptical about what and where improvements could be made to my agency however, he was right. Jonathan helped me to see what we were missing and clarified some of my thoughts and questions about how to improve things. I certainly felt more confident about making changes to our business with his guidance and reassurance that these things worked for him in his agency. We've since implemented a stronger business model which has helped us grow in size, client base, turnover and profit. Thanks to Jonathan I've not had a worry about the numbers for about 18 months and I feel much more confident about our future plans.

Liam

Not only has Jonathan been there, done that and bought the t-shirt - he's bought the whole wardrobe.
With over 30 years of experience in the agency landscape under his belt, Jonathan's a fountain of knowledge and we have access to his expertise through regular mentoring sessions.
Imposter syndrome is real, particularly when you're starting out in business. But with Jonathan's reassurance, we soon squished those feelings and felt fully equipped to follow our ambitions.
The insight he offers provides incredible value. We're now focused on growth and have the confidence to make decisions that build our business sustainably.
It's clear that Jonathan is driven by motivating and inspiring others and the years of hard work he's put into this book will undoubtedly have a hugely positive impact on its readers.

Courtney and Jess

Business coaches are like music producers. Without one, it's hard to make a great record. I've worked with Jonathan for just over a year. He keeps me enthusiastic about where we are going creatively, but also works deeply on the financial side to make sure we are profitable. He's very knowledgeable, professional and has helped our company focus on what we are good at.

Ale

Jonathan's coaching has elevated my design agency.
Since working with him my goals have changed, my mindset has become considerably more proactive and business focused, and the business has increased turnover, staff and profitability year-on-year. Having Jonathan's experience, knowledge and enthusiasm on-side has given me the confidence to take more calculated risks, become a better leader for my team and given me the belief we can continue to grow and succeed!

James

Before working with Jonathan our agency had sailed along quite well as a lifestyle business with 6 staff. We took the decision to grow and partnered with Jonathan as our mentor.
After 3 strong years of mentorship we are now 3 times the business we were previously, I can honestly say that having Jonathan in our business and at the side of me from a personal perspective has allowed every aspect of our business to bear fruit. We are now a stronger, more sustainable and financially secure agency with a clear vision.

Sean

It has been an absolute pleasure working with Jonathan as our agency business consultant. From our very first discussion, it was clear that his knowledge and passion for this subject afforded us an easy decision in asking him to work with us in growing our growing agency. After holding a fantastic workshop, he opened our eyes into a completely new way of working and how to extract the most of our existing client base. We look forward to a long and fruitful business relationship.

Richard

We started working with Jonathan at the height of the Covid pandemic so an uncertain time for business and we did question if this was the best timing to be bringing on an additional cost. I had an initial meeting with him when Libby, my business partner, was on holiday and I instantly thought he could be brilliant for us. We have worked with different mentors throughout our time in business but what really appealed to us about Jonathan was that he is from an agency background and has pretty much done everything we would love to achieve. We didn't know what to expect from our first session, but we both absolutely loved it. Not only does he bring valuable experience and advice, he is very down to earth and approachable. You can say literally anything to him, and we do! We are constantly learning and end each session feeling so positive, energised and excited. Jonathan has been a massive influence on our business and we can certainly see the changes he has installed in us for the better.

Jane and Libby

Being an entrepreneur can be a lonely place. The highs of building
a business and forging your own path can be incredibly exciting
but the lows of self-doubt, curve-balls and navigational pivots can
make the journey stressful by equal measure.
I met Jonathan at a transitional time in the business I had built alone,
from my living room, 4 years previously. It had evolved to become a
respected social media agency enjoying success with blue chip clients
and we were experiencing rapid growth moving out of start up mode.
Jonathan brought a level of experience that unlocked a deployable
strategy which I use not only in the evolution of my business (and the
operational challenges that come with it) but a change in mindset that
positions my business as the engine that fuels the long term ambition
in my personal life.
I can say with confidence that I am a more rounded entrepreneur
in my journey thanks to Jonathan's support and coaching.

John

Question: what do you get when you combine a rockstar with an astute
business brain? Answer: Jonathan Leafe, the man who has had the
biggest impact on my thought processes since Mark Zuckerberg in 2008.

Through spending regular, focused time with Jonathan, I was able
to go from having an agency business that could become something,
to a creative agency that really is something. He injected enthusiasm,
confidence and fascinating business insight that has enabled my
agency to change significantly, not only during the couple of years
he spent with us, but also in the time afterwards. I often find myself
thinking: "what would Leafe do?" when presented with a challenge,
and that usually helps me get to some fantastic solutions.
Many people say they're creative marketing rockstars, I've only
come across Jonathan who genuinely is.

Alex

Jonathan has helped to transform our business, as well as giving us a boost of energy, confidence and courage. The coaching, planning and mentoring sessions have created light where we had been operating in the dark, saving us time, money and years of learning the hard way. The results speak for themselves, with business almost doubling each year that we've worked together so far.

Greg and Lois

Jonathan is one of the most insightful, knowledgeable and valuable mentors in the agency world. His guidance generated an instant uplift in revenue for Skill + Fire. He's an excellent professional and a genuine, generous guy who adds tangible, real-world value. If you have a chance to get him batting for your agency, jump at the chance.

Jamie

Partnering with a mentor is one of those things you don't truly value until you have it. When we started working with Jonathan we had an inclination of where we wanted to go and how to get there but needed guiding through what has been a time of re-imagining both myself as a leader and the agency as a whole. Having Jonathan on board for the journey brought perspective, order and confidence to both myself and Sherwen Studios and we're excited for the future ahead.

Matt

CHAPTER 01

WHO IS THIS BOOK
FOR AND WHO AM I?

- Every agency owner that doesn't have a wealth plan
- Agency owners that don't have a plan that determines what the business may look like in 5 / 10 / 15 years
- Agency owners that don't have a plan that allows them the freedom to move away from the business without worrying about the impact on their income
- Agency owners that haven't got an exit plan

I've left until the last chapter to discuss the detail on 'I'm an agency owner get me out of here' because to enable you to do that successfully there are a lot of things that you need to get right well in advance.

But removing yourself from the day to day plan should start right now. The sooner you start to think about this, the better outcome you'll have.

In my work I have come across all kinds of agencies and agency bosses. They all have many things in common. Bearing in mind: Agencies are relatively easy businesses to start with little or no investment needed.

- But they are difficult to grow and hard to develop into decent sized businesses
- And, virtually no one who owns an agency will be able to sell it for what it's worth to them

However, it can be incredibly rewarding and tremendous fun building an agency.

I've set out to compile my thoughts on how to make agency life as easy and enjoyable as possible. I've used these methods with all of my clients and they've all benefited enormously. Increased profit, growing business, better life balance, calmer and a better understanding of how to be a GREAT agency.

Over the last three years I've helped numerous Digital Marketing and Creative agencies fulfil their potential with some superb success stories:

- One went from £-10k EBITDA to +£140k in 12 months
- One has nearly doubled their turnover and more than doubled their profit
- One went from having no retainer clients to 100% on retainers

The methods I'm going to share with you in this book are simple but they work. I'm not your average consultant either. I was an agency owner and specialist with over 35 years' experience, a mentor and a business expert.

ABOUT ME

I started my first Agency in 1989 and grew it to £2 million turnover with 40 staff before exiting in 2017 through a management buy-in by the senior management team. I had mentored them over a ten year period to enable them to successfully take-over - something that remains one of my proudest achievements to date.

My working life started somewhat unusual. I left school at 16 to work in the family business whilst simultaneously trying to become a popstar in a touring band in the very early 1980s. Being in the band taught me so much. Reliance on others, teamwork, creativity, practice, promotion, resilience, hard work and much more. It gave me a lust for life and a strong desire to be an entrepreneur.

After the band finished I worked in Southern Spain for a number of years marketing a hotel. In 1988 I saw my very first Apple Macintosh, which was why I started my first design agency on my return to the UK in 1989. I saw what was coming. Traditional agencies would be replaced by multi-skilled designers who would be able to create everything that where 4 or 5 people would have traditionally been needed and more quickly. It really was the start of the revolution that's still happening today.

This book is made up of the best bits of editorial, articles and blogs I've come across in my 40 years of working life, interspersed with my ideas, concepts and philosophy.

There are so many people I want to thank. My Mum, my late father, brother and sister and my partner Jo. All of them always believed in me and supported me, no matter what. And they pulled me out of a few holes from time to time too. Thanks also go to Sam Winsbury for editing.

My first boss in advertising, David Smith, and my colleague, Doug Davison. Both inspired me and taught me the ropes.

Finally thanks to my colleagues at Strawberry. I worked with both an amazing team and incredible clients who put their trust in me to guide them

More latterly, I'd like to thank all of the agencies that have trusted me to be their mentor, advisor and coach. It's an understatement to say that I've learned something from all of them. It's made me a much better, well rounded coach.

I thank all those that have inspired me to make (and write!) my own observations on these subjects. I now want to switch my focus to helping the next generation find the success that I did, and hopefully avoid a few of the pitfalls I didn't!

I've acknowledged content authors where known, others I acknowledge their copyright.

CHAPTER

02

HOW TO GET
TO THE MOON

HOW TO CLARIFY YOUR AGENCY'S MISSION

Before we get into the structure of agencies and how you can operate best, there are a few things you need to understand. If your agency is to reach great heights, it must have a clear mission, vision and set of values at its core.

HOW TO GET TO THE MOON

On 12th September 1962, the President of the United States, John F. Kennedy, stated in a very matter of fact way.

"By the end of the decade, we will land a man on the moon and return him to earth".

This is one of the world's best examples of a mission statement ever. It was definitive, time-limited and very specific. It was then down to NASA to deliver!

I'm constantly surprised that people run businesses without knowing where they are heading. The equivalent in the JFK example would have been him saying:

"We're going to build a rocket sometime in the future for a yet undefined purpose".

A successful plan should always start with what you want to achieve, and by when. Then, you have yourself a specific, desired outcome. From this desired outcome, you can then go right back to today and begin the planning phase.

NASA didn't go straight into building a rocket. They broke the problem down into its component parts and started planning around that. Once they'd reached a specification for each of those vital components, then they would start designing and testing each one.

Eventually, they would bring them together. The Saturn 5 rocket, with the Lunar Module on top, would take a man safely from the Earth to the moon and back again. No mean achievement in the late 1960s.

Let's translate this into a business scenario, specifically a marketing agency:

> ## IN 5 YEARS, WE WANT TO GROW FROM 5 EMPLOYEES TO 15 AND RETAIN 10 CLIENTS, SPENDING A COMBINED £500K, WHICH WE WILL TOP UP WITH PROJECT WORK TO THE VALUE OF £250K. WE WANT TO MAKE A NET PROFIT OF 20%

This is a measurable and well-defined goal, and is within a specific timescale.

Now, let's turn our attention to how this can all be achieved. This creates a level of focus, it oils the wheels of thought and prepares the business for its planned trajectory.

Whilst the route from A to B is never straight, and will undoubtedly bring setbacks, the core plan will ensure you stay focussed and keep as near to the track as you can.

NASA also had many setbacks. They were seeking to take men where they had never gone before - and this was by no means an easy journey.

As we all know, Apollo 11 landed on the moon on 20th July 1969, returning all three astronauts safely to Earth some days later.

This is actually much harder to define than it first seems. What I want to highlight here is that by reaching the end of this book it'll be a lot easier for you to define. But something to ask yourself now is why? Simon Sinek explains this incredibly well in his book 'Start with Why?'

THE GOLDEN CIRCLE

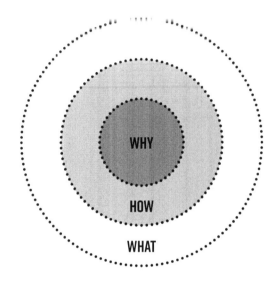

WHAT

Every organisation on the planet knows **WHAT** they do.
These are products they sell or the services.

HOW

Some organisation know **HOW** they do it. These are the things that make them special or set them apart from their competition.

WHY

Few organisations know **WHY** they do what they do. **WHY** is not about making money. That's a result. **WHY** is a purpose, cause or belief. It's the very reason your organisation exists.

WHAT IS YOUR VISION?

Again we'll come back to this later in the book. But think of this as your long term direction of travel for you and the business and what it'll feel like when you get there.

WHAT ARE YOUR VALUES?

At the heart of a great strategy are company values.
They make you who you are.

Values are not something that a marketer makes up. Nor are they something that sounds good to your employees. They're what you live and breathe. In essence, they're your 'brand'.

Th̶e̶ ̶j̶ ̶m̶ ̶i̶ ̶l̶ ̶t̶i̶ ̶l̶i̶ ̶ ̶m̶ ̶t̶ ̶i̶ ̶l̶ ̶m̶ ̶l̶ ̶i̶ ̶l̶ ̶i̶ ̶t̶l̶ ̶ ̶T̶h̶ ̶j̶ ̶m̶ ̶t̶h̶ ̶g̶l̶ ̶l̶i̶ ̶t̶w̶ ̶m̶ your company's teams and they're also what your customers rely on when they interact with you.

Values need constant attention to ensure that nothing drifts or changes which could have a damaging effect, or even a terminal one.

When something does go wrong it can be spectacularly bad for your businesses, with harmful effects for your customers, your employees and your stakeholders. The banking collapse of 2007-2008 is a prime example.

Often values come second to profit - but they absolutely shouldn't.

The business culture in countries such as Japan, China and India is to have companies which are still based on the values of their founders. These are views which have been held for many years, which in turn build long-term value and longevity. By contrast, choosing to chase the profit instead leads to short-term gains at the expense of long-term prosperity.

In my days of running a successful agency, I generated a culture based on values. During my time at the agency, I must have turned over a total in the region of £35 million, whilst also offering employment to 40 people at a time along the way. None of that would have been possible without a number of key values and practices.

- I never had contracts with clients - they could leave when they liked.
- My word was my bond.
- I always did what I said I was going to do.
- I tried my very best at all times for our clients.
- I treated their money as though it were my own.
- I nurtured a team that had the same focus as me.

I have also always held very strong values about supporting young people. Out of the team of 40, well over half had started their careers at Strawberry as either a graduate or an apprentice. I supported them with the belief that if they held the right attitudes and mindset, their skills would catch up soon enough.

If one left, I would take great pride in the knowledge that they had started their careers with us. It felt as though we were creating an army of advocates and ambassadors for the company. To this day, I'm still in touch with many of them.

We even set up a smaller sister company called StrawberryToo, that only employs first job graduates and apprentices. It was a tremendous success.

Our culture was projected outside the organisation too:

- We supported local, business-focussed organisations
- We supported charities and schools with cash, mentoring and pro bono work.
- We provided 48 weeks of work experience to secondary school students aged between 15 and 17.
- We provide paid internships to graduates.
- Finally, as had long been planned, I handed over the business to two directors that had been with the company, one for over 20 years and the other for over 10. I felt that the culture I had developed in the team allowed this to happen seamlessly and left the new shareholders with the best possible opportunity to have the same success I had personally achieved.

Did it work? Yes. Strawberry was and still is the largest full service agency to come out of Hull and East Yorkshire for nearly 40 years. It's grown in every year of its nearly 30 year existence and has made a profit every year of my stewardship.

The point here is not to shout about Strawberry's for the sake of it. It's to show what is truly possible when you place strong values at the core of your business.

"The assertion that 'female' companies will fare better in the 21st century than 'male' ones is an intriguing one - and one which can prove remarkably relevant for the modern company.

The basic notion that a company is able to have traits which can be categorised as 'male' or 'female' is naturally a tricky one. Of course, we are clearly stereotyping here - obviously not all men and women hold or exhibit the characteristics listed in this blog, nor are these lists exhaustive.

Let's begin with an exercise. Read the list below and tick all the traits that you believe apply to Apple, Google, Amazon, John Lewis and any other of the World's biggest companies that you can think of. Give them one 'plus' score for 'female' traits and 'minus' for 'male'. What would Apple's total score add up to for example?

'FEMALE' TRAITS

- Flexible
- Sincere
- Teamwork
- Honest
- Reasonable
- Cooperative
- Kind
- Listening
- Sensitive
- Gentle
- Adaptable
- Dependable
- Patient
- Supportive

'MALE' TRAITS

- Aggressive
- Rigid
- Decisive
- Focused
- Daring
- Overbearing
- Confident
- Straightforward
- Selfish
- Distinctive
- Self-reliant
- Direct
- Career-orientated
- Ambitious

Now do this with your organisation. How did you fair?

Were you leaning more towards 'male' traits or to 'feminine' ones? What are you going to do about it?

Obviously the best companies will have struck a good balance between the two - but out of both lists the most attractive traits are blatantly 'female'.

Or do you disagree? It's certainly something to think about. It's very subjective of course and it can be argued both ways but I've certainly come to the conclusion that this change has happened without any of us noticing - until now!

HOW TO BE LUCKY

I'm not a great believer in luck per se. I am, however, a believer in creating superior opportunities by being in the right place at the right time, being true to yourself and doing everything for the right reason.

Before promoting his senior soldiers to the roles of General or Marshal, Napoleon always asked the same question, "Are they lucky?"

If the answer was yes, they were promoted.

I came across the following list by Vala Afshar under the title '12 habits of lucky people'. It's absolutely spot on - and whilst I can't guarantee you'll be 'lucky', you'll definitely maximise your chances!

HARD WORKING

Fairly obvious this one. The famous golfer, Gary Player, responds to a spectator who asks him how he can be so lucky, by saying simply: "The harder you work, the luckier you get" - he was known for the hours he put in on the practice ground. I'm not suggesting that you start working 24 hours a day, so do not confuse long hours and hard work, as they are simply not the same. Hard work is about being committed and directing all your energies towards your goals. Long hours will sap your strength, make you disillusioned and forget your core purpose.

HIGHLY OPTIMISTIC

Are you glass 'half full' or glass 'half empty'? Optimistic people see opportunities everywhere. Pessimistic people see only the dangers that lie ahead and fall into paralysis as a result. This is not a good trait to have when seeking to increase your chances of success.

PASSIONATELY TEACH OTHERS

Those that pass on their knowledge without asking for anything in return end up with a highly motivated workforce and a solid network of colleagues. Ultimately, always remember that you'll be rewarded by the knowledge that you have helped others be the best they can be.

GENEROUS

Most 'lucky' people intrinsically know the difference between the cost of something and its value. You should always be prepared to show your generosity without 'counting score'.

PUNCTUALITY

It's not only a trait that will gain you respect, but it's also and that shows you too are respectful and that you recognise that it's not just your time which is precious.

A LOVE TO VOLUNTEER

Volunteering is good for the soul. It'll take you to places that you've never been to before and introduce you to people that you'd never normally come across. It enriches your life like you could never imagine.

STAYING TEACHABLE

Never, ever stop learning. The world is changing at such a pace that you need to stretch your mind every day just to keep up. Read voraciously, do things that take you out of your comfort zone, and set yourself daily challenges that will ultimately help you to become a better person.

GRATEFUL

No single person has achieved what they have without a close network of support around them. Family keeping you grounded, friends that support you, work colleagues that give you a sense of teamwork and belonging. Be grateful to all of them - they are the ones who have made you what you are!

PROMOTING OTHERS

Be open-hearted about others. Promote them more than you do yourself. Even competitors need promoting - they are the ones that keep you sharp and determined. It also shows respect and humility.

SEEKING RANDOM COLLISIONS

Spend time in places that you wouldn't normally go to, attend events that don't appeal to you. Serendipity has a strange way of working.

WELCOMING & KIND

There is no room for unkindness. To be heartfelt and welcoming to all (and to see the world from their point of view) will only advance your understanding of the world.

TRUSTWORTHY

To gain a reputation for being trustworthy, you must be trustworthy. In spirit, in thought and in all actions. It takes a lifetime to gain a reputation and minutes to destroy it.

I hope you've found my interpretation of Vala's list interesting. I have come across many very successful people in my time, and the vast majority of them display most if not all of these traits. Have another read through - how many do you feel you're currently fulfilling?

Credit - Lewis Kemp, LightBulb Media
Start acting like a B2C company. Stop treating customers like "leads" and start communicating like a human being:

• Let your audience see behind the scenes and get to know your team
• Run messenger campaigns
• Involve your target market in net promoter score
• Create content based on who you are rather than what you do
• Put a live chat feature on your website so your customers can speak to you in real-time

The vast majority of B2B businesses right now market themselves identically.

And the bar is incredibly low.

You really think people give a toss about the stale, compliance-laden bullshit you churn out saying how you're different from the rest?

You're not.

The only thing that makes you different from your closest competitor is your **TEAM.**

So don't strangle them with a corporate noose.

Yes, your company brand and your tone of voice are important.

But encouraging your staff to build their personal brands alongside it will supercharge your business growth.

Switch up your strategy and commit to it for 6 months.

CHAPTER 03

IN THE BEGINNING

WHERE YOU'VE COME FROM MAY DETERMINE WHERE YOU'RE GOING

WHO ARE YOU?

Are you entrepreneurial? Do you like to manage? What drives you forward? What are your good AND bad traits. How can you develop yourself?

It's always a good idea to understand what motivates you, what you like doing and what you're particularly good at.

I don't believe psychometric tests are 100% accurate - they should all be taken with a pinch of salt - but there can be huge value in understanding what they say about you and your team. Here are a few I like.

THE PERSONALITY CHART

I personally present very clearly on the second section, have some from the first section and some from the forth but hardly any from the third!

PERSONALITY TYPES

DOMINANT

- Powerful energy
- Direct communicator
- Very decisive
- Time & task oriented
- Natural leader

INFLUENTIAL

- Enjoys the spotlight
- Like to be liked
- Life of the party
- Warm & honest
- Natural talker

COMPLIANT

- Loves analysis
- Sticklers for the rules
- Often a perfectionist
- Reads the terms & conditions
- Naturally very accurate

STEADY / STABLE

- Loyal team player
- Focus on community
- Likes to research
- Calm & caring energy
- Natural supporter

This one is fun to do and very easy to access. I've done it on many occasions and always came out as ENTJ. But since I've started my coaching career I definitely shifted and now I'm most definitely an ENFJ.

ISTJ	ISFJ	INFJ	INTJ
Traditionalists	**Protectors**	**Guides**	**Visionaries**
11.7%	13.7%	1.7%	1.1%
Dutiful	Dutiful	Devoted	Independent
Practical	Practical	Innovative	Innovative
Logical	Supportive	Idealistic	Analytical
Methodical	Meticulous	Compassionate	Purposeful

ISTP	ISFP	INFP	INTP
Problem-solvers	**Harmonisers**	**Humanists**	**Conceptualiser**
6.4%	6.1%	3.2%	2.4%
Expedient	Tolerant	Insightful	Questioning
Practical	Realistic	Innovative	Innovative
Objective	Harmonious	Idealistic	Objective
Adaptable	Adaptable	Adaptable	Abstract

ESTP	ESFP	ENFP	ENTP
Activists	**Fun lovers**	**Enthusiast**	**Entrepreneurs**
5.8%	8.7%	6.3%	2.8%
Energetic	Spontaneous	Optimistic	Risk-taking
Practical	Practical	Innovative	Innovative
Pragmatic	Friendly	Compassionate	Outgoing
Spontaneous	Harmonious	Versatile	Adaptable

ESTJ	ESFJ	ENFJ	ENTJ
Co-ordinators	**Supporters**	**Developers**	**Reformers**
10.4%	12.6%	2.8%	2.9%
Organised	Friendly	Friendly	Determined
Practical	Practical	Innovative	Innovative
Logical	Loyal	Supportive	Strategic
Outgoing	Organised	Idealistic	Outgoing

Based on a collection of psychometric tests, we can characterise the following personality types within agencies.

MANAGERS

- Research & analyse
- Develop business plans
- Hold meetings
- Write reports
- Follow procedures

LEADERS

- Get into the zone
- Create superior opportunities
- Marshall resources
- Build capability
- Achieve results
- Achievement drive
- Vision
- Energy
- Action oriented
- Savvy focus
- Positive counsel
- Self determining
- Persistence
- Passion
- Experiential learning
- Staying on track
- Recover from setbacks

WHAT ARE YOUR BEHAVIOURS?

TRADITIONAL MANAGERS: LEFT BRAIN

- Research & analyse
- Plan
- Have meetings
- Write reports
- Set budgets
- Make presentations

LEADERS / INNOVATORS: RIGHT BRAIN

- Getting into the zone
- Seeing possibilities
- Staying in the zone
- Opening up to the world
- Building capabilities
- Creating superior opportunities

TRADITIONAL FIRMS: POWER & CONTROL

- Bureaucracy
- Systems
- Politics
- Planning
- Rule compliance
- Analysis
- Formality
- Order

ENTREPRENEURIAL FIRMS: ACHIEVEMENT

- Autonomy
- Ownership
- Risk taking
- Breaking the rules
- Informal
- Synthesis
- Intuition
- Trust

SECRETS TO SUCCESS

Reckon you've stumbled across the next 'big thing'? Believe there's definitely a market for what you're selling? Think you'll be better or that you have a unique selling point?

This could all be blind optimism. Your friends and family will no doubt offer words of support and encouragement, but don't mistake that for usable market research - only a fool would use it as the basis for a successful business.

I've worked with hundreds of start-ups and I can pretty much tell if they have a chance within five minutes of talking to them. There are four types:

- A great entrepreneur with a good idea
- A great entrepreneur with an OK idea
- A bad entrepreneur with a great idea
- A bad entrepreneur with a bad idea

Only the first two have a real chance of success. Number 1 will usually have a knowledge of the market that they're going into, as well as a deep understanding of the problem that they're trying to solve. Finally, they will likely have an intuition as to the value they offer to their clients.

Number 2 can still be successful. I've never met a good entrepreneur that had only one idea. Good entrepreneurs are characterised by their open mind, can-do attitude and resilience. Sometimes, all they need is a mentor to tease out a new idea.

Spotting bad entrepreneurs is fairly easy. They're often blinded by their insistence that they're right, yet have nothing to back their ideas up. They're often arrogant and will show little resilience to setbacks. Even if they have a great idea, they're doomed to fail unless they hand over development of the business to others.

In summary, to be a successful start-up you need to have the following four traits:

- Confidence in both your abilities and your idea
  (but never arrogance or blind optimism)
- Resilience to carry you through the inevitable setbacks you'll encounter
- Attitude: be open-minded at all times. Never, ever stop learning
- Persistence: do not stop at the first, second or third hurdle
  Where there's a will, there's a way

However, having these four traits alone will not be enough.

It might give you the sling shot and adrenaline to get going but to stay in business and to grow, you'll need to get a team together. That requires leadership skills even great entrepreneurs lack.

This is where a good attitude comes into play. You need to be open-minded and appreciate that you don't know everything and never will - you need to be continuously learning.

Having the right attitude can be turbo-charged by mixing with the right people, I'm a founding member of a brilliant organisation, For Entrepreneurs Only, which is based in Hull, East Yorkshire. This is the only organisation that I know of where the members pay to join and then donate their time to helping others become more successful. It's helped literally thousands of people to start up, develop and then refine their business with the one aim of helping the economy of East Yorkshire to thrive.

Oh, and you need a bit of luck too — every business does!

HOW AGENCIES FORM

Most agencies come into being by one talented freelancer joining another, getting a few good clients who then in turn need to hire staff to cope with the influx of work. Fast forward 12 months and they're now a team of 5 or so people and they're an agency!

But this comes with inherent dangers. Mostly, the original freelancers are great at what they do but lack the required management and business skills. Some will pick up the extra skills, learn to delegate, see that they need to grow the business to ensure stability. Others won't. They'll lurch from project to project, never being able to get off the tools, because they're the most skilled. It's a merry-go-round.

WHICH AGENCY ARE YOU?

Marketing and Creative Agencies are fairly easy to categorise. Whether you're in digital, design or marketing, chances are you'll recognise yourself here.

STAGE 1: 0-3 PEOPLE

› 55% OF AGENCIES

Easy stuff this. You're a good designer and/or marketer and have a few contacts, so you decide to start your own agency and hey presto, you're off! Overheads are low, confidence is high, you love doing what you do and you can work where and when you like. The trouble is, since this seems like a perfect place to settle, you may well be here forever. It's a stage with pitfalls too, as you'll find that holidays are difficult to take and new business is hard to secure.

STAGE 2: 4-8 PEOPLE

25% OF AGENCIES

You're clearly good at what you do. You've found your niche and people want to work with you. New business comes along too, but you often have a tendency to focus your work solely on these new clients and forget to look for further new business. This stops you from growing.

STAGE 3: 8-12 PEOPLE

15% OF AGENCIES

You've found a client you're growing with. They keep giving you more and more work, which seems brilliant - though you start to realise that they're dominating your workload. Since you're working well with them, and you're still growing, you end up focusing all your energy on advancing their business.

This means new clients are potentially reluctant to come to you, because you're overwhelmingly under the thumb of this dominant client. New opportunities pass you by, never really getting the attention that they merit.

However, Stage three can be a great place to be. It's an easy to manage place with predictable revenue and you're still on the tools and doing a bit of managing. But in all reality it's not going to provide any wealth in the long term. You're more of a turbo-charged freelancer.

STAGE 4: 12-30 PEOPLE

5% OF AGENCIES

You're an agency of some size now - a big player. You've crossed the threshold of being just a collection of people. Now you're organised into teams with clients that have stayed with you for some time. You're not overwhelmed by one dominant client, instead working with a handful of large clients, many medium-sized clients and an abundance of smaller ones. You've settled on the processes, disciplines and specialisms with which you want to work, all of which allow you to predict where your revenue will sit, your possible profit margin and an idea of where you can grow with some accuracy.

However, the pitfalls remain. You're struggling with talent recruitment issues, not to mention that all the local competition want to knock you off your spot. As a result, you need to constantly pitch for new business, whilst still maintaining client confidence and satisfaction.

Because of the resulting need for more business structure, overheads become higher, and management and financial structures are necessary.

You've also had to make the transition from an on-the-tools worker to a business owner. Not something that everyone wants to be. But it will provide you with the platform to create significant wealth for you and to build a legacy.

STAGE 5: 30+ PEOPLE

1% OF AGENCIES

99.5% of all agencies will never get here. It's rare, particularly if you're away from a big city. But the economies of scale kick in and profitability may well come back.

To maintain this position you need to have a USP, otherwise agencies in all of the above categories will sneak onto your blindside and take you on. Key staff may leave and form their own micro agencies and take your clients and / or staff, irrespective of what it says in their contracts. It can be a real minefield at this stage.

STAGE 6: GET ME OUT OF HERE

This is seldom achieved, with a financial exit usually on the cards. I'm very confident that most, if not all of you, will be able to identify with at least one of these six stages.

Being the boss or owner of an agency is hard - very hard, especially when clients and staff become increasingly demanding.
Approached in the right way, however, and it can prove a very rewarding experience. With the right guidance and the right resilient mindset, anything is possible.

When the exit does come and you're ready to move on don't think that you'll just sell-up, as will be discussed at the end of the book. It's not that easy. It's reckoned that only 1 in 400 creative businesses actually achieve a trade sale.

The pot of gold waiting for you at the end of the rainbow may well not be there.

Often agencies grow on the back of their successful clients who feed them more and more work. Quite often this puts the agency in mortal danger. If anything should happen to that client they're in trouble too. So by definition agencies must grow and find new clients and potentially offer new services.

But beware - there are ways of doing this. The classic Ansoff Box highlights what to do and what not to do.

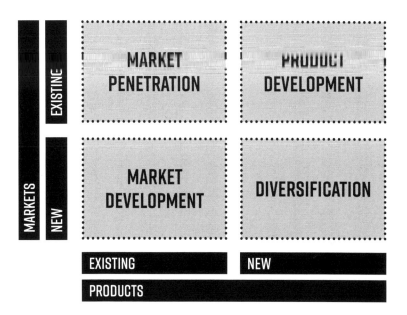

Market development is the easiest and safest way to proceed, at least initially. Find new clients, ensure that they know what you're looking for and go get them.

As you grow and establish a balanced client base you can - and definitely should - grow the amount of business that you get from your existing customers. This could be finding out what services you offer but they don't take, upselling or product development. Diversification, though, is expensive, risky and to be avoided.

CHAPTER 04

FINDING THE
IDEAL CLIENT

FINDING YOUR TRIBE

Thank you to Helen of H&H Agency for this wisdom.

Thinking tribal is a really effective way to get momentum going.

There are lots of different buzzwords to describe this marketing process... relationship marketing, purpose driven marketing, movement marketing... but we'll stick with the expression tribal marketing

The need to be part of a tribe is directly linked with our basic human need to belong, and it has been programmed into us from our cave dwelling days. The worst thing that could happen to you in those early days of human development was to be banished from the tribe. You would almost certainly die.

Knowing a need for belonging is in our nature, marketeers have used it really effectively to build brands and businesses. You might not realise but most of your buying decisions are made from deep rooted needs and genetic programming.

But what does buying this say about you? Which tribe do you want to belong to?

For example:

- Are you an Apple person or a PC person?
- Are you a Coca-Cola person or a Pepsi person?
- Are you an Everton or Liverpool fan?
- Are you a vintage clothing person or a latest fashion person?
- Are you soul and R&B or are you heavy rock?

Every decision you make defines which tribe you see yourself belonging to, because you share similar values and beliefs. This is the essence of a tribe.

There is absolutely a tribe of people waiting for you to connect them. To allow them to belong to something meaningful. To connect them with other like-minded people.

Your job is two-fold. First to decide what your tribe stands for. And second to find your tribe – the group of people who will absolutely buy into what you believe and what you stand for.

Having a belief in something more than just selling 'stuff', is what builds tribes.

People don't buy benefits and features any more – that's old school. They buy into how your product will make them feel about themselves. They buy products from the companies that share the same beliefs as them. This is what turns them into fans and builds loyalty.

Tribes become fans - not just customers. You need fans if you want your business to grow.

Customers are fickle. Fans are fanatical. In the business world today, it's not enough to have customers. You need to create a fan-base of loyal people who totally get what you're about. They'll stay loyal. They'll tell others about you. They'll offer you support and guidance.

Fans will go out of their way to buy from you, recommend you, and invest a little more to support you. Because they believe in you and what you believe in.

THE CHECKLIST

Agencies are often guilty of inviting every possible type of client into the business.

Every new client is good, right? - WRONG!

I used the following as a ready reckoner to see if the client I was speaking to fitted my criteria of what a good client looks like.
The real benefit of doing this is actually two fold. One you get the client you deserve and the client gets the agency they deserve.
It's basically a compatibility test

You should make your own to suit yourselves, but this is mine.

Calculating a lead score:

HOW DID WE GET THIS LEAD?

Fundamentally, if you know someone well you'll be able to have a much better, more in-depth conversation about the work that needs to be done and if you're the right company to do it. If the lead comes in as a general

Recommendation or cold lead then it's going to be a lot harder to do this (and successful onboarding is going to take much longer).

- We know this person well - 5
- We know this person - 4
- Recommendation by trusted advocate - 3
- Recommendation - general - 2
- Any - 1

TYPE OF PROJECT

There's no doubt that the best customer is one that either retains their work with you or comes to you on a regular basis, maybe every week, month or quarter. These are much more predictable when it comes to forecasting and it allows you to layer your business for growth. Big projects are also fine of course, but there must be something afterwards. I'll discuss this in Chapter Six.

- Retainer - 5
- Regular - 4
- Big project - 3
- Small project - 1

TYPE OF PROJECT

Fairly obvious but worth scoring as there may well be not so profitable opportunities but the very nature that you've actually done work for the company or brand brings great recognition which you then leverage.

- Financially profitable - 5
- Fun to do - 4
- Will make us famous - 3

TYPE OF CLIENT

The only client to have is one that looks at you as a partner in whatever you're doing. They rely on your advice and your service helps them succeed in business. Once you slip into supplier status, that client could leave at any time for any reason.

- Collaborative and partnership focussed - 5
- Wants supplier relationship - 1

POSSIBLE SCORE OUT OF 20

Add the score up and choose how to proceed. As I said before, if they score highly it's because you're also going to be great for them to. Share this methodology with them - they'll be very pleased you did. But please do walk away. Getting the wrong clients in the agency will cause you pain. You know this to be true - we've all been there.

- Above 16 - go get it
- 11-15 - consider it
- 10 and below - walk away

THE RELATIONSHIP

Like any relationship there will be ups and downs and it's always a little bit exciting in the first few weeks and months as you get to know each other and the first work is delivered. But like any relationship, it can go stale pretty quickly if you don't commit to work on it. You must at every stage understand the client's objectives and make sure that what you offer and do fulfils that.

If you get a client that tells you what to do, you're a supplier.
If on the other hand you listen to what the client wants and then deliver what the client needs, you're in a partnership. Which will last longer? Which will provide more income for the agency? It's pretty obvious.

43

Much of my work for clients is focussed on making sure they understand what the client brings to the agency. I use a simple league system. If you follow football (soccer) you'll be familiar with it, but it's very easy to understand: Premier League, Championship, League One and League Two.

Which league clients are in is not solely dependent on how much money you bill them. You should also consider:

- Are they fun to work with? Do they bring joy to the team? Is their work exciting, creative different?
- Do they treat us as an expert partner?
- Are they an 'Energy Vampire'? Does everyone in the team want to be off the account, are they overly demanding, do they constantly change their minds, do they send briefs at 5pm on Friday?
- Profitable - do we use the hours we predicted more or less?
- Are they growing or in a growth industry?
- Do they have additional potential for us?
- Are they with us for the long haul?

Clearly any client scoring well in those lists would go straight into the Premier League. Equally you can't have every client you have in that top division - you actually are better off with a spread. The only one to really watch and avoid is the 'Energy Vampire' who is resource hungry but won't pay for extra.

The best decision I ever made was sacking a client who was a classic Energy Vampire. It was a large part of our turnover as well at the time. In reality, I think we looked at the revenue and forgot everything else. None of the team liked working on the account as they were often demanding, unreasonable and a huge drag on senior management resources. I sacked them and replaced them very quickly with some new clients that treated us well.

I read a blog by a very well respected Digital Agency Consultant and he maintained that all agencies should go hunting more. I fundamentally disagree. Hunting even sounds wrong to me.

If you're a start-up, perhaps you have no choice. But if you're established then you should be nurturing your clients. Working with them to develop their businesses. Going to them with new ideas not waiting for them to come to you.

There's always at least 20-50% more revenue in your client base that you've simply not tapped into. This is Farming. Farmers know that to grow a strong crop you need to look after the land. Agencies are no different.

With existing clients you can pick up the phone and be in a meeting with them soon and be talking about new opportunities you have found for them. They'll be grateful for you coming up with these ideas and more often than not they'll agree and you've won more business and developed an even happier client.

The vast majority of clients that walk away from you is because they feel you're ambivalent to them. They're not daft - if they see you actively hunting, they'll realise that they are not so important to you.

A hunter needs to be hunting all day long with no guarantee of a catch at the end of the day. And when a 'potential' opportunity comes along the tendency is for the hunting agency to put the A team on the pitch and leave their B teams to service their existing clients. This is not good at all.

This approach is often described as inviting new customers through the front door and watching existing ones disappear out the back.

Or being in the bath with the taps fully on with the plug left out. **Do not let this be you.**

To get the business opportunities you need to be a magnet!

We'll discuss this in Chapter Seven.

CHAPTER

05

THE TRIANGLE
OF HAPPINESS

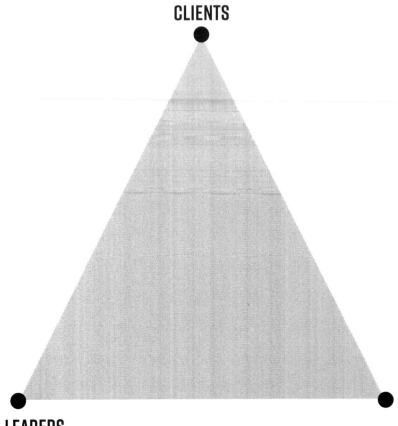

CLIENTS

LEADERS MANAGEMENT OWNERS

TEAM

To become a GREAT company you need to have everything in balance. You have to have the right clients into the business, you have to have the very best team you can assemble and you have to demonstrate fantastic leadership.

But fundamentally you have to start with what's in for me? This is not an exhaustive list but it helps you think your way through this.

WHAT DO CLIENTS WANT?

- Great work
- A fair price
- A good service
- Someone that they trust

WHAT DOES THE TEAM WANT?

- Interesting work
- A secure job
- A fair remuneration
- Career progression
- A good boss

WHAT DOES THE LEADERSHIP, MANAGEMENT AND OWNERS WANT?

- A smooth operation
- A high standard of work
- A good return on their investment
- Predictability

All of these are entirely compatible and it's at the gift of the leadership and senior management team to make this happen.

Depending on the size and structure of the agency, it may well be that the management, leadership and the shareholders are one and the same - and their needs are definitely related.

Let's begin with a classic miscommunication example that is used in most marketing and communication schools.

The story goes that the commander of a battalion on the Western Front radioed to HQ to ask "Send reinforcements, we're going to advance". This was grossly misheard and misinterpreted, with potentially disastrous consequences. "Send thrupence, we're going to a dance."

In military terms, miscommunication also caused absolutely carnage in the ill fated Charge of the Light Brigade.

Thankfully, we have better communication technology now. And that should, in theory, allow us to negate errors in basic communication. However, this is sadly not always the case.

Poor use of language, being verbose in communication and not being clear on the question you're asking or the request you're making will lead to misunderstanding.

The great communicators over the years have learned to be brief and very specific when outlining what they require from their opposite number. The greatest of them all was, of course, the Duke of Wellington. He reputedly said, "To write half as much takes me twice as long."

He always remembered to give only the most concise of orders to his commanders, so that they were entirely unambiguous and direct.

Airline pilots have also been known to use a universal language that is, much like the Duke of Wellington's communication style, designed to avoid misinterpretation. Any errors here, and the consequences are catastrophic.

Fortunately, in most of our lives miscommunication does not end in disaster or death. But, believe me, it can. So, the next time you write any Fortunately, in most of our lives miscommunication does not end in disaster or death. But, believe me, it can. So, the next time you write any email, regardless of its importance, think about how it will be read, and whether or not the language you've used is concise and unambiguous.

Here are my top tips on how to avoid these errors in everyday and business communication:

- Use simple and universally understood words
- Be clear with what you want. A reply? An action? When do you need it?
- Be polite but brief
- Short sentences
- Limit adjectives
- Take your time to write it
- Pause before sending and reread and check
- Would your granny understand it?
- Do not copy everyone in – it devalues the message
- Good luck!

CHAPTER

FROM NABLA TO
TOWER TO PYRAMID

BUILDING A SUSTAINABLE AND SUCCESSFUL AGENCY

If you want to build an agency that is not only profitable, but also sustainable long term, you need to establish multiple income streams and handle them each differently.

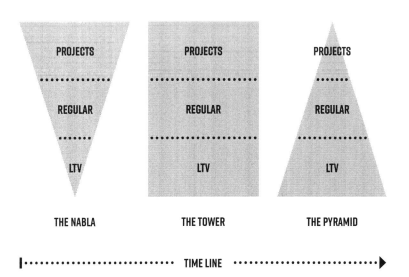

THE NABLA   THE TOWER   THE PYRAMID

Most agencies in their first few years will be in the upturned triangle or 'Nabla' phase. Most of their income is generated from new projects and new clients but this must change quickly to build a sustainable agency. After a few years their income breakdown may look like this:

- Projects - 65%
- Regular or retained - 25%
- LTV - 10%

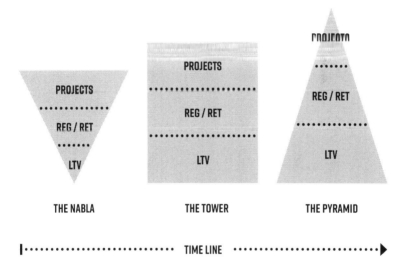

THE NABLA   THE TOWER   THE PYRAMID

TIME LINE

This is not sustainable - it's too risky. What if your projects all dry up or all come at once? There's no structure and no easy way of growing the business.

Moving from The Nabla to The Tower is easier than it may seem.

You make the move by selecting the right clients (the ones that come to you for a project must have something else afterwards). In the case of a Digital Agency it may initially be a website, followed by a technical, service level agreement with plans to maintain and work on the project through development or content and some critical asset maintenance LTV (Life-Time-Value) income.

After another few years the business income breakdown might be:

- Projects - 35%
- Regular or retained - 40%
- LTV - 25%

This is much more sustainable and the 'predictable' income of the business is now nearer the 65% mark. If you were to follow this trajectory you'll arrive at The Pyramid.

Here your income streams may look like this

- Projects   20%
- Regular or retained - 50%
- LTV - 30%

Predictable income is now close to 00%. This is much more sustainable and puts you in a really strong position. If you make 20% net profit, you break-even without any new business.

Assuming new project work stays the same throughout, you've actually managed to grow the business by 3.25 times! If you grow the new project work by double over the period the business will be 6.5 times larger. This is classic layering and nearly all agencies are capable of doing this. You just have to change how you think.

WHAT IS A PROJECT?

Projects are customisable and often bespoke.
Most agencies start with a new client on a project basis. This is fine, but not sustainable forever. Projects, by nature, have a start and end. They are characterised by phases.

THE DOWNSIDE OF A PROJECT

Being bespoke or customisable means they very rarely have a defined outcome. Even if they do they are subject to feature bloat and mission creep - both of which harm or damage your profitability. I would even go as far to say that most projects are not profitable.

Projects demand senior management input to stand any chance of success and this is often where agencies get bottlenecked. Resources are thin on the ground as it is - projects suck in even more staff time, resources and management.

Most agencies are not set-up to manage a project like an IT company would, for example. They manage it with an open-ended brief that changes as the project progresses.

It's critical that the vast majority of your projects are ones that lead into other more sustainable revenue. That's where the value and scalability lie.

WHAT DOES A WORLD-CLASS PROJECT LOOK LIKE?

- Phase One - **Scoping** - Few clients ever really know what they want.

- Phase Two - **Specification** - This has to happen. Miss it out and you've left the door open for massive mission creep and feature bloat. This will happen anyway but if you have a blue-print, at least you can go back to it and challenge the client.

- Phase Three - **Design** - Drafting the look and feel.

- Phase Four - **Build** - Putting it all together.

- Phase Five - **Alpha release** - Internal testing.

- Phase Six- **Beta release** - Client testing.

- Phase Seven - **General release**

- Phase Eight - **Review and iterate V.1.X.**

- Phase Nine - **Tech support and long term value**

- Phase Ten - **Conversion Rate Optimisation and User experience improvements**

- Phase Eleven - **traffic building**

- Phase Twelve - **V.2**

Building and maintaining a World Class Website, Custom software or E-commerce Project

NB - Once a gate / phase is closed it cannot be reopened unless the project is stopped and reviewed

	Description	Spec & Design	Build & Test	Release	Market & Optimise
Phase 1	Scooping - bearing in mind - few clients every really know what they need in detail - investigate user stories etc.	•			
Phase 2	Specification - this has to happen - miss this out and you've left the door open for mission creep and feature bloat. This will happen anyways but if you have a blue-print at least you can go back to it and challenge the spec.	•			
Phase 3	Design - Drafting the look and feel and User Experience (UX)	•			
Phase 4	Build - Putting it all together / this can be further broken down into detailed build parts if known / identified		•		
Phase 5	Alpha release - Internal testing - amongst the close agency and client team only		•		
Phase 6	Beta release - Full client testing / limited number of trial users		•		
Phase 7	General release			•	
Phase 8	Review and iterate to Version 1.01 - 1.X etc			•	•
Phase 9	Tech support				•
Phase 10	Employ constant Conversion Rate Optimisation (As a service) / split and UX testing				•
Phase 11	Marketing and traffic generation				•
Phase 12	Version 2.0				•

I would strongly advise that you do not finalise a fixed price until after Phase Two is completed. And you should most definitely charge for the specification. If the client has objections to this, agree that at the end of the specification phase they can take the specification to other agencies to complete it. In reality they won't of course.

If you're very skilled at managing this you will have already discussed the ongoing phases - to move it into a V.2 and have a Technical SLA in place to support it. It's worth also discussing and fixing the asset support in place.

I've yet to come across an agency that makes significant profits on projects. By their nature they're time-consuming and hard to manage. There will always be some mission-creep and feature bloat - it's expected. And if you're not protected or sharp on this - your costs will overtake what you're charging very quickly indeed.

However, if you have retained technical and asset support built into the overall then these are areas that are generally very profitable and recurring. Indeed if you have a marketing team then you should already be deploying your services on this too for more retained revenue. The advice here is clear - slow down to speed up. Do not let the client run the project. Whatever project or development management system you use - follow it!

If you manage this then you're well on the way to building a better business.

WHAT IS A REGULAR OR RETAINER CLIENT?

A client that uses you on a regular basis or is on a fixed monthly retainer. These types of clients need to be run without any or little intervention by senior management. When designing how you handle this business you must establish systems and processes to manage them. Ideally, one size fits all is the place to start and make slight adjustments per client if needed. But remember the more adjustments you make, the less profitable they will become.

WHAT IS LIFE-TIME VALUE INCOME?

Once you have established a client through a project to retained work, you have to have a third income stream which looks after itself. In the case of a development agency this may well be hosting, emergency technical support (as required) and asset management. This should be managed by an automatic process that needs virtually no intervention from senior managers or even staff. It should be a recurring income that just happens. This income will be the most profitable in the agency.

There are many articles that criticise universities on the basic premise that, at the end of a three-year course, whatever you learned in your first year becomes obsolete. A challenging and intriguing proposition.

Another common argument points to the fact that many of the jobs which today's children will go on to undertake do not exist, or have not yet even been imagined.

This is nothing to be alarmed about. In fact, the chances are that you will identify with either both of these statements, or at least one of them.

The world changes every year. Sometimes, these changes are dramatic and obvious, whilst sometimes those changes are more subtle. Take, for example, space flight as a dramatic and obvious change, compared to car design or the internet, which both involve more subtle alterations.

Space flight represents groundbreaking innovation, whilst car design and the internet involve changes and improvements of a more incremental nature. Groundbreaking innovation needs big R&D budgets, extreme risk-taking and, of course, nerve. Incremental changes need a rolling process of business improvement and an open mind to change.

For example, take a car model that changes and improves its features, efficiency and design every three years by 25%. In a decade, it will be an entirely different car. The changes, however, are all relatively subtle, and we wouldn't necessarily notice them unless the two different models were placed next to each other for a direct comparison.

Every successful business should be, at the very least, micro-innovating every year. New processes, new staff, new services, new markets - all of these can and should be considered.

By doing this, you'll always have something new to offer your existing clients. They'll be pleased that you're ahead of the game, and feel relieved that you're not suggesting the same solutions to the new problems that they've encountered.

The by-product of this is that you'll be able to keep your profits up. Selling obsolete services that can be compared to others offered by your competitors will only push the price down and your stress up!

Successful businesses use this knowledge and formula to progress. They may not be groundbreaking or known for innovation, but they stay in business for a long time, become more profitable than the average organisation, attract the best talent and increase their client base.

I once spent a very rewarding day with the ex-Chief Executive of a £4 billion pharmaceuticals business. He said that they spend enough money on R&D to ensure that over a three-year cycle, at least one third of their inventory is new. This ensured that they always had new products to take to a first-world market that was looking for innovation, a market that could afford their products. Their older products, which had been copied or become generic, could still be sold into the third world markets at a price that was competitive and profitable. This business is now almost 170 years old!

The key thing to take away from this is that change is essential to keep a business successful. Any successful leadership team needs to have an open mind and an attitude across the team that recognises this as essential.

Innovation happens slowly. Most engineers will overestimate the speed of progress over the next few years, and dramatically underestimate how much will be achieved over the next decade. Why?

Let's take an example. If change happens at a relatively slow rate of 5%, and a compound effect change is taken into account for the next couple of years, we're looking at a rate of between 10 and 15%. Examining this over the next decade, however, and it's a different story. We'd be dealing with an innovation rate upwards of 65%.

A car purchased 10 years ago will have fewer safety features than one bought today, and will be significantly less economical too. Technologically, it'll be unrecognisable by comparison.

Securing innovation right at the core of your business is vital to being able to survive and thrive. There are three steps to making this happen:

STEP ONE: LOOK AT YOUR BUSINESS DATA

Customer purchases, repeats and confidence. What do they all tell you? What's happened? Some might see this as market research, but it's not. It's a historical view of what worked and didn't work in the past.

This is an essential first stage of the process.

STEP TWO: LOOK FOR THE TRENDS

Analyse each facet of your business using this data, and take note of what is going up and what's on the way down, in whichever way works best for you. An effective technique would be to score each out of 10 (10 being for a strong trend with a great future and 1 for anything on its last legs).

There are countless examples here. Take one of the most innovative pharmaceutical companies in the world, with 30% of its products being newly developed every three years. They look at the 8-10 scored trends, using the scale above, and develop new products aimed at these trends before they become mainstream.

This secures an advantage for the product in terms of price and attractiveness as they reach the market first. These are markets mostly aimed at first-world countries that can afford the prices for products offering such innovative qualities.

The products that score lower do so because they've been around for a long time. Competitors have caught up and are able to challenge these products on both price and quality. The scoring system here allows the company to recognise that further development of these products is redundant.

STEP THREE: GROUND-BREAKING INNOVATION

In this stage your focus has to be on the weaker areas in the marketplace, and on where the world will be in three to five or more years' time. This is anticipation and is easier to achieve than you might think.

Often innovation is linked to what others are doing. Take, for example, electric cars. These are nothing new. In fact they precede the internal combustion engine, which has stayed at the top of the tree for a century. We can anticipate that this is about to change, however, with the traditional engine set to be knocked off its perch.

Softer signals have already been apparent. Among other similar incidents, the VW scandal involved trying to fix emission data, with diesels causing pollution on an invisible yet monumental scale having created a disillusionment within the marketplace.

However, for this innovation and progress to come about, battery technology had to improve, and it did.

Now, it's moving to become mainstream and will accelerate as car manufacturers state their claim to the new territory. Tesla has moved fast and are very much in pole position, whilst all others are now following. Perhaps we'll see an Apple or Google 'car' in five years' time.

To aid this innovation, however, the Government will need to ensure that charging points are as widespread as petrol stations. This is no 'quick fix' and could turn into what is essentially a catch-up job when we consider the sheer pace of the progress in the electric car industry.

The innovation model explored here offers a fruitful alternative to R&D, and can be applied to any business in any industry. The change required is only a small one, and is one of mindset.

Often, it is those on the outside of your business who can spot the trends and areas crying out for change.

Imagine yourself driving a car and looking only at your rearview mirror. It's almost certain that you're going to crash very quickly. It would be much safer (and wiser) to look at the road ahead rather than the one behind.

Why is it that so many businesses look only at the past to try and inform the future? Whilst looking back can play a role to some extent, it should by no means be a prevailing atmosphere or attitude.

There appears to be a recurring trend among marketing agencies and many businesses out there to conduct market research through data driven decisions, with some calling this 'big data'. It's research that leaves you like a rabbit in the headlights, without seeing what you need to.

'Big data' can be overwhelming. It's a technique which captures significantly more information than is needed, and leaves you in a state of paralysis, excessively analysing fine details which will have little bearing on the big picture.

Agencies and businesses conducting this market research often stop innovating, mimic the competition and play it safe. This leaves your communication with customers safe, uninteresting and bland, with the strong likelihood that you'll lose them altogether.

Your current generation of customers will drift away and the next generation of potential customers will bypass you. It's game over.

MOVING AHEAD:

You need to have your eyes beyond the horizon. If you're not updating, changing, or upgrading over 30% of your products and services every three years, you're moving backwards.

So what can you do to stop this? The first step is straightforward and essential:

STEP I: ORGANISE YOUR DATA

Get a simple dashboard which brings all of the data you collect together into an easy-to-digest format. This is what will highlight the trends you need to see - information that will keep your business going for the next 12 months.

STEP 2: LOOK OUTSIDE

Spend at least 10% of your time reading about the best businesses in their fields - not yours. The best buyers, the best manufacturers, the best tech companies. What do they know and do that you can bring to your organisation? Taking this on board will leave you with a significant advantage over your competitors.

STEP 3: LISTEN

Talk, listen, listen some more and then listen some more.

There are faint signals out there which will give you a glimpse into what's coming ahead of you and ensure your organisation is agile, innovative and already there in the future, whilst your competitors are still looking in their rearview mirror!

Look forwards, not backwards. Look outside of your business, and outside of your industry. And listen to the signs - this is how you prepare for, and embrace, what's on the road ahead of you.

5% IMPROVEMENTS CAN MAKE A LOT OF DIFFERENCE

I challenge my clients to make small improvements all the time. Little changes that will tweak and polish the business. And they should be doing this constantly. Many believe that business development comes from dramatic changes. This is not so. It comes from micro-improvements that, when compounded, make a huge difference.

For example, if you improved your business by 5% a month after a year it will have been improved by 80% - a remarkable transformation. This can be done by your agency.

- Select an area for improvement
- Appoint a champion
- Create an achievement culture
- Find new perspectives
- Trial and error pilots
- Leverage success
- Learn lessons

The key is consistency. You must always be doing this. You cannot stop.

CHAPTER

07

BECOMING MAGNETIC: GET THE RIGHT CLIENTS FOR YOU

STOP PITCHING AND GET CLIENTS COMING TO YOU

PEOPLE ARE ATTRACTED TO POSITIVITY

Going through life with a good attitude will make you much more successful. It's as simple as that (plus you'll enjoy the journey more too!).

People with the right attitude are open-minded and learn more easily. The right attitude will allow you to metaphorically, climb walls, jump over hurdles, navigate through storms and ultimately get to your destination without too much fuss.

Here are a few things to remember when It comes to developing your new, enhanced attitude:

HOW TO LEARN BETTER

- Read more
- Write more
- Memorising is not learning, doing is learning
- Ask better questions
- Practice public speaking
- Effort matters

Learning is very important to developing a good attitude. It allows you to see the world from somebody else's perspective and to respect that others may have a different view. Reading blogs or books on the subjects of psychology, business, marketing or sales will enrich your mind - see what you can get your hands on!

When studying formal subjects, don't memorise them as though you were studying for an exam. Immerse yourself in the topic instead.

Ask the questions that aren't obvious - especially the ones you don't know the answer to. Others will be delighted that you're interested and will revel in helping you.

Practising public speaking is a great way to organise your thoughts. Imagine that you have the stage whilst everyone else is listening to you - now is not the time for waffling or winging it. A well-prepared and succinct presentation delivered with enthusiasm and a smile will always win the day.

Always remember that no one got lucky without putting effort in. The more effort you put in, the luckier you'll be.

HOW TO NETWORK BETTER

- Find a mentor
- Networking is about giving
- Collaborate more

Networking is what makes us who we are, whether you're developing friendships or business connections. It's an interchange of knowledge, experience and expertise given freely and unconditionally. It promotes collaboration and puts you in a position where you'll constantly be learning and developing.

It helps make the biggest difference of all to your attitude: belief in yourself.

As Rudyard Kipling put it in his poem 'If', "If you can meet with Triumph and Disaster, and treat those two impostors just the same."

Developing a good attitude is something you need to work at. It comes from a combination of being optimistic and pragmatic at the same time. It's about taking joy in the smallest and largest of things. As Kipling wrote, it's about treating triumph and disaster as if they were equals. It's about being resilient under pressure, getting back on the horse after you've been thrown off.

KISSING A FEW FROGS

You will kiss many frogs on your business journey.

I used this to generate my Master Checklist of the most desirable type of client to get into the business. After a while you do learn, but you must learn because the minute you start to look at the value alone of a potential contract you lose sight of your mission, vision and values.

SIGN-POSTER

These are an incredible source of leads. All you need to do is ask. When you are speaking to clients and you have a new service, a new employee or even a new idea... why not ask what your 'loyal' client thinks? If they like you they'll be only too happy to make introductions for you.

CHAPTER

08

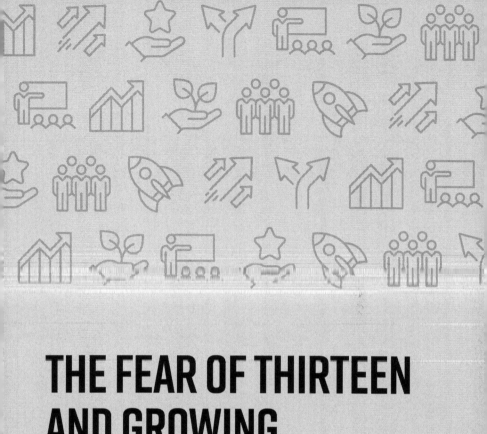

THE FEAR OF THIRTEEN
AND GROWING

WHAT TO EXPECT WHEN YOU GROW

THE FEAR OF THIRTEEN

Twelve is a beautiful number. You can see everyone. You understand all their strengths and weaknesses. You know what they're working on and when it needs to be done. Ultimately, you can tell whether they're doing a good job or a bad job.

Your turnover is in excess of £500k, and you're seeing a very decent profit too. The business is stable, predictable and life is good. Now the question lingering over you is, "Do I twist or stick? Do I go for growth or consolidate?"

This isn't the only question that will confront you. More will circle in your head until you come to a definite decision. What will happen if one of your biggest clients goes or key staff leave? What happens if a competitor comes up on your blindside and starts winning all the new business pitches?

Many owner-run agencies get stuck at around twelve team members. It's a pivotal moment in the life of the company, and one where you need to make a big decision: whether to go for it or manage decline.

The truth is that neither option is correct. Both are valid strategies and your decision will depend on which you personally want to pursue.

Let's take a look at the options:

PATH 1: GO FOR IT

Be prepared for a rocky time. Be prepared to cross the desert, to be disillusioned, to sleep less and to endure the change from being a 'manager' to an owner. These are two very different places to be.

Growing the business needs structure, processes, procedures and discipline. It needs senior staff and it needs a clear chain of command.

You need a watertight strategy, and a solid company culture which you have designed (you'll get one anyway, and if you're not in control of it - beware!). You need to have a clear vision and solid values. You need to have the next tier of managers ready. Who will replace you? What is your exit strategy? You need to read, observe and take in what the best businesses do. You need to think like a PLC

But there's one key thing to remember above anything else. You need to let go to grow!

I know - this is a lot to take in. Incorporating all of these strategies and ideas can feel overwhelming, and this is why so many agencies don't even start the process of growth.

But what happens when you've finished crossing this desert?

The agency is now in the 'Premier League'. It's profitable, it's predictable and it's stable - but on a much greater level than before. Now, you can start to look at the agency as an investment vehicle for your lifestyle and your exit strategy.

PATH 2: MANAGING DECLINE

This is by no means an unreasonable option to choose. You keep your overheads low, you continue to maintain the client relationships yourself, and you may even do a lot of the work yourself too.

However, there's no exit plan. The business is you, and because of this it's really not saleable. You may have a family member who'll take it on at a stretch, and there may even be a team member who'd be capable of taking it over - but how will they afford to buy you out?

At best this is a lifestyle business, not a pension plan.

So the choice is yours! Cross the desert or sit in the comfy chair - whichever works best for you.

CHAPTER 09

THINKING LIKE
A GENERAL

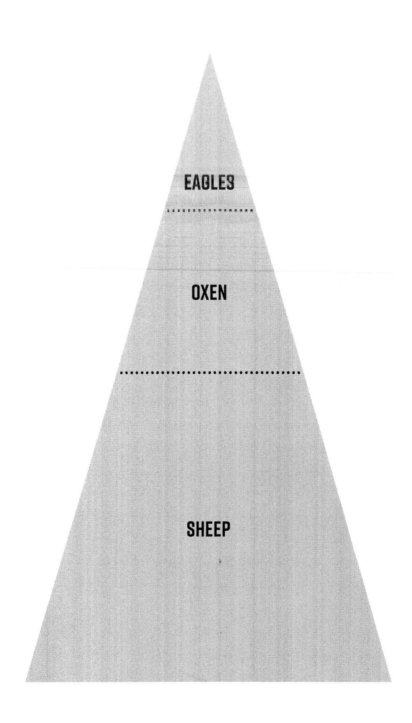

EAGLES

OXEN

SHEEP

WHICH ARE YOU: A SHEEP, AN OX OR AN EAGLE?

James Sinclair brought up this concept in a vlog and I really liked it. Most businesses are run by Sheep (that's fine by the way). Many people get into the agency world because they're good at something and develop from being a freelancer into a business owner after employing a few people but they don't change how they operate.

Representing 60% of business owners, Sheep are consistent. They get up, go to work, waiting for the telephone or email to ping and they're off doing work. They measure their success (if they even do that) by the amount of orders or jobs they've done and return home satisfied and ready to do it all again tomorrow.

The Ox, representing 25%, however, measures their success by the number of hours they do. They'll not be happy until they've pushed on through 80 hours a week. They'll fetch and carry, jump on the project as they're the only ones that can do it well, fight the fires, carry the large loads even though they have staff to do these things.

What you want to be though, is an Eagle. Eagles let go to grow, delegate effectively and lead the team. This allows you to focus on the strategy, the direction, the important issues that only you can do.

Another way to organise is this is your task list. Take out a piece of paper and write down all of your tasks and grade them from 1-10.

Anything between 8 and 10 is an Eagle task and only you can do it.

Between 5 and 7, delegate and stay in the loop, but do not do it!

Anything lower than a 5 should be delegated and left for it to be done.

Your list should dramatically shrink and leave you with a clear purpose.

77

Generals are usually chosen for their skill in fighting wars and battles, but there's more to being a general than meets the eye.
Finding similarities in the attributes of great generals and great business leaders is, somewhat unsurprisingly, not a difficult task.

Take two Generals from the early 19th century, Napoleon and Wellington, both of whom were very successful, each adopting and utilising their own unique leadership style, richly different from the other.

Napoleon on one hand was charismatic, energetic and daring. Wellington, however, was cautious and reserved. Napoleon would not involve himself in the detail of the army, leaving this instead to his marshals. He'd outline the strategy himself before letting his marshals to execute it. Wellington, on the other hand, would be very precise with his orders, leaving his generals very little room for interpretation. He famously remarked that it would take him "twice as long to write half as much". His orders were concise and succinct.

Napoleon once said that "if he had enough ribbon he would have conquered the world". He would lead from the front and reward the bravest soldiers with medals, honours and promotion. He trained them to be agile and move fast, living off the land and relocating quickly. Napoleon would take advantage of any mistake his foes made and be quick to react and capitalise on them, often before they even knew it was happening. This gave the French Napoleonic Army an air of invincibility, driving the armies of Europe before them (all apart from the British army).

Wellington was totally different. He was a calculating general, looking months, if not years ahead, to defeat his enemies. He was a meticulous detail planner and would involve himself in every aspect of running the army. He would establish supply routes, before ensuring that his army was always well provided and accounted for, never risking his men unless he was absolutely sure of victory. Perhaps his soldiers didn't love him as Napoleon's loved him, but they respected him and would always do as he asked. He trained them well and the vast majority of his army were volunteers (if not slightly coerced from time to time).

I would consider Napoleon's to be an entrepreneurial-style of business leadership, with a willingness to take risks. He's very much a 'brand' man. Think Richard Branson as a modern example - thinks on his feet, good with one liners. You know what you're going to get.
Steve Jobs would also fall into this category - much more of a maverick leader than most.

Wellington could be characterised as an effective Chief Executive of a long standing and successful PLC. Virtually any CEO of a FTSE 100 company would fit into this character. By nature they need to be steady, reliable, be able to answer to shareholders and the City.

Think of a few bosses and leaders that are around today - which ones are they?

Personally, I have tried to adopt a little of both. Napoleon's innovation style and Wellington's attention to detail. Bearing in mind Napoleon's career was over by 1815. Wellington went on to become Prime Minister and a confidant to Queen Victoria. His career outlasted Napoleon's by a significant number of years. Who would you rather be?

CHAPTER 10

WHO'S ON THE PITCH? BUILDING THE DREAM TEAM

"WHENEVER I SEE A SUCCESSFUL BUSINESS THERE IS ALWAYS A SWITCHED ON TEAM BEHIND IT."

Tom Peters

It's very obvious that the right team will make all the difference to your Agency's performance. I was very lucky I had an amazing team and I seemed to be good at finding them. I made a few mistakes as well. When you do recruit it's important to check two things out. I did separate interviews for this and got different people in to do them.

First was the culture test. I never had a CV in front of me – the CV had got them through the door. By this stage the work they had done at school, college, university and in the previous jobs had got them this opportunity. I only wanted to find out what made them tick. I would ask myself, will this person fit into our culture? Will they enhance it and will they grow? How keen are they to work for my company? A keen volunteer is worth 10 pressed men!

If the answer was yes, I did my very best to sell my company to them. This has to be a two-way process.

The second interview was the competency test and this was conducted by the very people who would either be working with them or their line manager.

If both interviews went well they would be offered the job.

Once you've given them the role, your job isn't finished. There are a few other important things to ensure you do:

- Take care to induct them into the culture of your business
- Ensure they are very clear what is expected of them
- Provide any necessary coaching, training and development
- Provide feedback on performance
- Reward them for their efforts

Constantly be recruiting. You never know when you're going to need somebody, and you'll never find someone when you're desperate either. So I think it's perfectly okay to have your recruitment always active. If someone turns up unexpectedly that you simply can't turn down, hire them!

The old adage goes that you should always by trying to replace yourself with better people. You have to be prepared to let go to grow.

DEVELOPING THE TEAM

Any team needs to be developed and nurtured. It is not enough to employ them, plonk them at a desk and let them get on with it. All staff, junior to senior, need to be guided, mentored and encouraged. And regularly too.

In any organisation you will have three kinds of employees.

20% will be the entrepreneurs of the team. They'll be the ones with the ideas to drive the business forward. If you haven't already these need to be identified and given special attention. These people need constant encouragement and care needs to be taken to keep them on board. Ultimately they will make the biggest difference to your agency. But resist the temptation to keep hiring entrepreneurs - any more than 20% will result in chaos!

70% will be the ones who do the majority of the work and keep the ship afloat and travelling in the right direction.

10% will not be engaged, for whatever reason. These people need to be identified and encouraged to get out of their comfort zone, or to get out of their rut and start developing again. Watch for those who move into this category.

BUILDING THE TEAM IS ABOUT COACHING - ADAPTED FROM KARL SAKAS

A Harvard Business Review article describes four reasons managers make time to coach their employees:

- They see coaching as an essential tool for achieving business goals
- They enjoy helping people develop
- They are curious
- They are interested in establishing connections

That first point—about coaching helping you reach your business goals—is key. You're helping yourself as much as the team.
(H/T to Casey Cobb on the article.)

- **Build a baseline.**
  Start by understanding where people are now. In learning, people start at the delightfully-named 'unconscious incompetence', which is a fancy way of saying, "You don't know what you don't know." You need to know what they know and what they assume. This baseline gives you an opportunity to adjust along the way.

- **Talk about their goals.**
  What do they want to learn? Where do they want to go? The key is to ask questions and then listen. In my experience, some employees will be more forthcoming than others. Sometimes people aren't sure where they want to go. In this case, you have an opportunity to help them figure that out. Sometimes people are concerned about job security if their true goals don't fit their current job. In this case, you need to create a safe space for people to share. Better to help people find a new role—at your agency or otherwise—than have someone stay for years when they're not engaged.

- **Talk about company goals.**
  Do people know where you want to go and your values in getting there? They should anyway, but it's especially important in coaching. Your team is more likely to help you meet your goals if they know your goals. People want to understand how they fit into your agency's future.

- **Find ways to align your and their goals.**
  Ultimately, you need them to meet your agency's goals, but think about how your and their goals align. For instance, someone might want to get experience in event management, and you need someone to organize an upcoming event—sounds like a promising overlap. In cases where there isn't overlap—say they want to learn a skill that's unrelated to their work—think about ways they can fulfil that need outside of work, through volunteering or other opportunities. This is part of why I encourage agencies to allow employees to freelance—it's a "safety valve" to do things they can't do at work.

- **Make a plan.**
  Don't over-complicate it. Only focus on a maximum of 3 major goals each month—you can juggle only so much. The plan should have concrete goals, with deadlines. Senior employees will have further-out deadlines, with monthly or quarterly check-ins on those goals. Junior employees might be working a month or two at a time, with weekly or biweekly check-ins.

- **Help them find their own resources.**
  You can suggest resources—for instance, agency PMs should read Interactive Project Management and Project Management for Humans, and agency account managers should read The Art of Client Service—but the real goal is to teach people to find their own answers. Maybe it's a lineup of industry blogs, or people to follow on Twitter, or certain online communities. When they can find resources on their own, you go from teacher to coach—which is a more scalable shift as your agency grows.

- **Check-in regularly.**
  If you set goals and never talk about them again, you aren't doing people any favours. Schedule check-in meetings now—you need a standing meeting. Consider meeting for coffee or in another setting outside the usual office, to shake things up. Make employees responsible for sharing their progress and bringing a list of questions for you. You're busy—you're there to facilitate, not micromanage. Manager Tools recommends weekly 30-minute "one-on-one" (O3) meetings.

- **Don't reschedule.**
  Don't reschedule coaching meetings. Your team is what makes you an agency owner instead of an individual marketing consultant. Everything you do to help your team has a multiplier effect—getting them moving in the right direction and doing it better means they're accomplishing things while you're elsewhere. Do everything you can to avoid rescheduling internal coaching meetings.

- **Decide how far to take things.**
  Some people just aren't a fit, no matter how much coaching you provide. In those situations, set a timeline for improvement. At the end of the timeline, decide whether to continue—or to cut your losses.

  You'll need to adjust your approach as you grow your agency. You can coach everyone if you have 10 employees. If you have 20-25, you'll focus on coaching your direct reports. If you have 50+ people, you'll spend your time coaching your directors on how to better coach their direct-report employees.

HELPING EMPLOYEES WORKING OUTSIDE YOUR SKILLSET

A client mentioned it's easier for him to coach his designers—he started as a designer himself—than to coach his developers, project managers, and marketing strategists. That's understandable, but you have some tools available for helping employees outside your skillset.

Get advice from colleagues who do understand the work. Maybe it's a fellow agency owner who knows that area better. Maybe it's your business coach. Maybe it's a more senior team member doing similar work. If you're a non-technical person managing technical people, read Managing Humans: Biting and Humorous Tales of a Software Engineering Manager. Ultimately, you need to understand enough

Ask employees to explain things to you in ways you can understand. This is harder when you have junior employees (the "unconscious incompetence" problem I mentioned earlier) but frankly, you shouldn't be hiring junior people if other people at your agency have no understanding of their role. Using a "throw them in the deep end" recruiting approach leads to lots of mistakes on your agency's time.

Commit to studying management. Management isn't entirely interchangeable—there are common skill sets, but it's harder when you don't understand what your employees do. Ultimately it's about sharing your vision, giving people long-term goals, and removing blockages to let people get things done. Don't use "I don't understand what they do" as an excuse.

Whether you consider yourself to be a creative or not, being able to be 'creative' is now one of the leading skill requirements that employers are looking for - and this is the case in more industries than you may think.

The world is moving so quickly that innovation is paramount to all organisations. Bosses want people that are adaptable, can think on their feet and can contribute to the success of the organisation rather than simply employees who turn up and shift metaphorical boxes around.

So getting 'in the zone' and being able to stay there is a skill. It can often feel like a daunting challenge for the creative type. But it's not as difficult as you might think.

The world's greatest creatives hardly ever invent something brand new. Most creativity comes off the back of something else. What they do is take existing concepts and make them much better by tweaking them and making them their own. Some may call it plagiarism, but that's uncalled for. It's simply creative evolution.

Ask a creative type a question, simple or complex, and they'll more often than not come back with an answer much bigger than expected. Creatives look to scale up ideas, are unafraid of making a mistake, and ultimately believe that you can't be too bold. You can always scale back ideas, but it's nigh on impossible to expand them. As the old adage goes:

HOW TO LET YOUR CREATIVITY SHINE

- Be very observant
- What's the best similar example that exists?
- Get out of your comfort zone
- Be fearless
- Don't ask for too many opinions
- Be flexible, but only a bit
- Think it through
- It'll never be perfect, accept that
- Work quickly - often the best idea is the first!
- Polish but stop tweaking

Hopefully this has helped you consider how you approach being 'creative'. Remember, this is a lifelong challenge, offering the richly positive side-effect that, in striving to be creative, your mind gets stretched all the time.

CHAPTER 11

WHAT TO DO WHEN IT STOPS: ESCAPING THE FOG

This is a very nice analogy from DENT and Daniel Priestly. Most businesses experience 'getting caught in the fog' and not knowing where they are or where they should go next.

This is very common. Businesses start life in a wave of euphoria, optimism and expectation. The first years are full of opportunity, growth and excitement. Plus you've got the energy to match that atmosphere.

After this initial period, things inevitably start to slow down. Clients don't renew their contracts. They become slow payers and cash flow becomes an issue. Projects start to go awry and business ideas that you had or products and services you've launched just don't turn out as you'd hoped. You become tired. You're in the fog.

This can happen anytime in your first five years and if you're not ready and don't have the energy or resilience for it, it can be terminal.

It can also creep up on you and be very disorientating. Sometimes it can actually be overwhelming. Speak to any business owner and they'll recognise this.

At this stage many business owners think, "Sod that - I'll go back to the start where it was pain-free and enjoyable". You'll try and get back to why you started the business in the first place. This is a really bad thing to do. You may think that trying to retrace your steps is a sensible strategy, but this is what will take you deep into the fog. And next time, you won't survive it.

The way to survive and get through the fog is to look at what you have. What's good? Do more of that. What's bad? Why is it bad? Think about what you can do to improve it. The key is to keep moving forward.

A practical way to determine what's working and what isn't is to make a list of all your products, services and the type of clients that use them. Then take the different client types and group them into logical families, before giving them each three scores out of ten.

The first one is for profitability, the second is for longevity (i.e. how long you think people will still want this service), and the final - and perhaps most important one - is how often people want it (i.e. will they buy it often). Then, follow the scale below:

- 25-30 - this is where you need to be focussing your attention to climb out of the 'fog'
- 15-24 - this area needs reviewing, but shouldn't be your primary focus.
- 0-15 - think about dropping this group, and dropping them immediately. You need to move forwards, not backwards

This is the mindset and process that you'll need to follow, over and over again. Each time it will get easier. Your resilience will become polished, and you'll be ready to cope with being in the 'fog'.

RESILIENCE

For any business owner the greatest skill you will have to learn is to be resilient. No one is born with it and whilst some take to it more easily than others, resilience is key to long term success. Wherever you are with your career or business development it's worthwhile reminding yourself what you need to do to become resilient.

Resilience can come from a number of different places.

YOU

- Be optimistic and patient
- Find a sense of purpose in your life
- Look after yourself
- Establish achievable goals

YOUR WORK

- Build positive beliefs in your abilities
- Develop your problem-solving skills
- Never stop learning
- Embrace change

YOUR ENVIRONMENT

- Develop a strong social network
- Do things that challenge you
- Dismiss energy vampires

YOU

The YOU part is perhaps the hardest. It begins with having a positive, can-do attitude. The type of optimism that, no matter what the circumstances are, can put a smile on your face. If you can achieve this without thinking about it you'll find a sense of purpose in your life. But to effectively do this you need to be patient. Not everything happens at once and you may well need to go down a few cul-de-sacs before you find what you're looking for.

In the meantime it's essential you look after yourself The mind is a complex machine that lives in a fragile body and unless that body is looked after, the mind will never work properly. So spend time exercising,eating well and healthily and getting the right amount of sleep.

Achievable goal setting will also give you focus and direction. There is no point setting goals that are so elevated that the realistic chances of them being achieved are slim. However you should always set goals that are slightly outside your comfort zone. This will both stretch you and give you a sense of achievement.

WORK

You have to be realistic about your capabilities. Focus on what you're good at and be honest about what you're not good at. This way you'll build a confidence that is unbreakable. You can always polish what you're really good at and minimise what you're not. But the first revelation is knowing that.

Being good at problem solving is essential to building resilience. Problems will always emerge and challenge you. Take them head on, viewing them as challenges to be solved rather than something to worry about.

No matter how good you are at something you can never stop learning. Rapid advances in technology have ensured that nothing remains constant and change is part and parcel of life. This will only accelerate further. I say embrace it and keep your mind supple by learning something new everyday.

ENVIRONMENT

You are what you are surrounded by. The people you have as friends, the business colleagues you know. Each one of those will support you unconditionally provided that you do the same for them. This is not scorekeeping either. It's giving you, your time and your efforts selflessly and with an open heart.

From time to time you must get out of your comfort zone and do something that is challenging to you. It will add a sense of achievement, build confidence and core resilience. It tells you are capable of anything.

Lastly, get rid of the energy vampires in your life. You know who they are. They're the pessimists, the impatient, the glass half empties

MENTORS

Everyone needs a mentor. And everyone's had one, even though they may not have realised it at the time. Whether it be your mum or your dad, your aunty, your uncle or your teacher. There are people from your past that have guided you to become who you are.

A good mentor doesn't tell you what to do. They help you make your own decisions and avoid the pitfalls they've experienced. A great mentor helps you become the very best version of you, you can ever be.

In business the most valuable member of your extended team is your mentor and they can appear in many places. It may well be that you have more than one mentor too.

In my career, I've had many. They are people I love listening to. They may be work colleagues, clients, business associates or friends. They all have their own story and unique perspective. Listen carefully, there's alway something you can pick up.

How do I think big? I listen to people who have been there and done it. Established business people who have really succeeded where others haven't. How do they act, what do they say, how do they conduct themselves. What traits do they have that set them apart? Ask as many questions as you can. No need to hound them though!

How do I keep in touch with young minds? Volunteer at schools, talk to junior staff, ask them what they like to do, what they think about current events, how they are affected. It's eye opening and adds to your understanding of the world as it develops.

How do I learn from the past? Ask older people. They have experiences that you'll never have thought possible. It's humbling to hear how different their lives have been to yours.

How do I improve myself? Talk to spiritual people (they don't need to be religious either). You know who they are, they're the wise ones, the ones who are calm, maybe slower moving than you. They have a deeper perspective on the world than you'll probably ever have.

How do I keep myself enthusiastic? Avoid the energy vampires, the glass half-fulls, the ones that see shadows where others see sunshine.

"

YOU'RE WELL OVER HALFWAY THROUGH, ALMOST THERE!

HOPE YOU'RE ENJOYING THE BOOK SO FAR.

JONATHAN

"

CHAPTER

12

CLIMBING
THE MOUNTAIN

For over fifteen years, every year I've challenged myself to do something different. It really doesn't matter what it is either. But it's important. As an agency boss it's very easy to get caught up in the routine and the daily battles. Having an escape keeps your mind supple and allows you to stay objective.

So far:

- I've climbed Kilimanjaro
- I'm sprucing up my Spanish
- I learned to Scuba Dive • I'm now a master scuba diver
- I recorded a new album with my group from the eighties and played 6 concerts
- I've run three marathons, three half-marathons and 10 x 10ks
- I've walked the gruelling Yorkshire Three Peaks twice
- I've learned to do the Rubik's Cube (PB 2 mins 30 seconds)
- I've volunteered to be mentor at my former school
- I'm now a governor at my former school
- I'm a trustee of a charity
- I've been to a cocktail party at Number Ten
- I've been an invitee at The Buckingham Palace Garden Party
- I've attended functions at The Palace of Westminster on numerous occasions
- I got back into going to concerts
- I downsized my house to get nearer to my friends
- I upsized my house to live with my girlfriend and three cats

WHAT DO I WANT
TO ACHIEVE?

01:

02:

03:

04:

05:

06:

07:

08:

09:

10:

CHAPTER

13

I'M AN AGENCY OWNER GET ME OUT OF HERE

Here's a 'bring you back down to earth' fact - Only 1 in 400* marketing agencies will ever be bought out. And those that do tend to be specialist, high margin and with a high turnover.

*According to the highly respected 2 Bobs podcast.

That doesn't mean you can't exit successfully. But if you're chasing the pot of gold at the end of the rainbow and relying on that to fund your retirement - please don't!

That's why I came up with the solution - I'm an agency owner, get me out of here!

At some stage you may well want exit, here's how:

- Trade sale
- Management Buy-out
- Management Buy-in

I planned to sell my business 10 years before I managed to do it. My plan always was to exit by the time I was 55, to give me some time to develop my last career of mentoring, consulting and advising, which I thoroughly enjoy.

COMPARISON OF EXIT ROUTES	UPSIDES	DOWNSIDES
Trade Sale	Potential biggest sale price	Length, due diligence, lock-in
Management Buy Out	Quicker process	Capital to buy you out
Prepared Management Buy In	You're in control	Length of time needed to prepare

Only 1 in 400 agencies will be bought out!

The problem with agencies is that, as previously mentioned, they rely on three things for success. A great client base, a superb team and an astute leadership team.

This doesn't make an attractive trade-sale though. Clients can be fickle - particularly if they rely on the senior management team, staff tend to leave more often after a takeover and the leadership often is the one that's selling. You can see where the difficulties lie.

The situation is exacerbated if the seller is heavily involved in the business. **Are they actually the business itself?**

What then are your options? A trade sale is the one that stands out in the media. But these are incredibly rare for SMEs because of the aforementioned reasons. The only time when this may happen is if the agency has a **special niche and/or specialism** or **marquee clients** that the buyer would like to have. Perhaps this would provide a quicker route into a niche territory for the acquirer? Perhaps there's even some unique or intrinsically valuable IP at stake too? That could be particularly attractive.

Another aspect of a trade sale is that there is a mountain of due-diligence that needs to be done and this can take months. It's extremely distracting (and expensive). Often, once completed it'll highlight areas that are weak and the buyer might exploit those for a cheaper price. If there's an earn-out and the company doesn't make the profits, set in the sale budget, then you can also be penalised as well - this really does happen!

You may also have a lock-in for a number of years where you work in the business as an employee with effectively a new boss. Which could be challenging for an entrepreneur or someone is used to working for themselves. Even after you have left there may well be a non-competition clause for a number of years which effectively precludes you working in the industry after you've exited.

A trade sale is the dream of many agency owners, but sadly the reality is that it is often only a dream.

If you wanted to follow this route I would highly recommend engaging with a Business Sales or M&A (Mergers and Acquisitions) agency.

They don't come cheap but worth every penny as they'll find the right buyer, if there is one, and get the best price for you (hopefully one that sees what you see!) Waypoint Partners are such a business - but their entry point is a high Gross Profit and an equally high Net Profit.

MANAGEMENT BUY-OUT

A management buy-out is similar to a management buy-in but with the subtle difference that the management are approaching you to remove you. They are in the driving seat. The pay-out and terms may be better than a buy-in. This is actually a great way of doing it because in effect the senior management team and clients don't change. The only change is you move out.

The downside is that they will have to find the capital to buy you out on whatever deal is negotiated.

MANAGEMENT BUY-IN / SUCCESSION PLANNING

My favoured way is the management buy-in. But as I mentioned before you need to start this well in advance of the target sale date - as much as 5-10-15 years, as I did. To get the maximum value out, you'll likely need to build up the cash reserves.

But let's be clear about this. As an SME agency owner it's highly unlikely that you'll come out with a life-changing amount of money, so make sure you have things in place for your future: a great pension pot and an idea of what you plan to do next (depending on your age and energy level).

To realise the value in this takes time though, because you have to replace the capital you have in the business with other sources. That may be personal loans, business loans or other kinds of debt. Ideally not leaving the company buy-in in a precarious position due to being too heavily in debt. Don't worry, this is easily achievable.

There are government backed schemes to help with employee ownership, such as EMI (Enterprise Management Incentive).

I chose my successors a full ten years before I exited. It's not essential that you allow ten years for it to happen but the longer you give it, the better.

The team member/s that you identify as being the ones that will take over are often fairly easy to identify. They already are contributing to the success of the business. They've got the potential to grow and learn. Be careful though, just because they're good at their job doesn't mean that they're going to be good at running and developing a business, nevermind being the boss and managing the team. If you select the right people you have time to coach and mentor them. Getting them on a fast tracked path to equip them to be ready to take on the business when you're not there.

As such I like to drill down to what a plan could look like.

This is my start point. It shows you how the 'buckets' of wealth need to look as we progress.

SAVINGS	HOME	BUSINESS	PENSIONS
TARGET SAVING	EQUITY	TARGET EQUITY	TARGET EQUITY
TARGET SAVING	EQUITY	TARGET EQUITY	TARGET EQUITY
TARGET SAVING	DEBT	EQUITY	TARGET EQUITY
SAVING	DEBT	EQUITY	EQUITY

SAVING	EQUITY	EQUITY	EQUITY
TARGET SAVING	DEBT	TARGET EQUITY	TARGET EQUITY

◀ ···| ····················▶

TAX INEFFICIENT   **TAX EFFICIENT**

Phase one is for those in their 30s to early 40s.

To get under way you need to know where you are financially. There's a great tool to use - https://www.moneyadviceservice.org.uk/en/tools/budget-planner/start. This will let you see how much money you need to sustain your lifestyle.

- **Personal** - How much money do you have in **savings?**
- **Personal** - How much **mortgage** do you owe over how long? How much is your property worth?
- **Business** - How much equity is there in your business? What are the **shareholders funds?**
- **Pension** - How much is there in the **personal pension** and when do you want to retire?

With this information to hand you are now at the start of
your journey. Ideally, you'll do this at least 10-15 years in advance
of your retirement / exit.

The next checklist is about how much you want to have at exit point.
The key is to be realistic with this. The longer you have to plan the
greater the chances are that you'll reach your goal.

- How quickly can you pay off our mortgage?
- How much can you pay into your pension fund monthly/yearly?
  At present you're allowed up to £40k per annum
- How much surplus profit can you leave in your business pot?

Getting money out of a limited company and paying the least amount
of tax is vital. Capital gains tax will be payable on any share that you sell
But there are Government scheme criteria that entrepreneurs who exit
their business.

You need to earn enough to sustain your lifestyle and the one that
you aspire to. But once you start paying the higher rate of tax, it's very
expensive! A quick note here to say if you have a spouse you might
consider using their taxable allowance too. Anything to avoid paying
the higher-rate of tax and to add to their pension pot too.

However, saving into a personal pension paid through the business is
extremely tax efficient and saves the company any national insurance
payments too.

Also reducing any debt - i.e. your mortgage, is also key - paying your
mortgage off early will save you literally £000s.

It's important to run through these plans with your company
accountant and get the best financial advisor you can.
They'll help you work through detail.

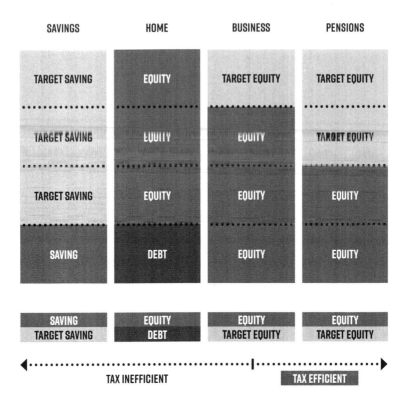

Phase two is for those in their late 30s to mid 40s.
Nailing your target wealth plan.

Once Phase One is established and working, start to work out how much you can grow your pots of wealth and over what timescale. Overlay this with what you actually need at the end of the project (retirement/moving on). This will inform how much wealth you need to generate to satisfy your needs.

It's a fine balancing act between supporting your lifestyle, debt-reduction, long term financial planning and a successful business exit. The one thing that makes it all work though is the success of the business. That's where we create wealth.

A rule of thumb is to work back from your retirement (pensionable age).

Say you're 45 now and you want to exit when you're 55. It's 67 when you can draw your pension and you need an income (which doesn't rely on the business or any other work) of £50k per year after tax.

So you need to be (very roughly) putting in £40k per annum into your pension

You need to be adding approx £60k per annum onto your shareholders' funds

At exit you'll be left with £500k value in the business which you can draw down on at a tax rate of 10% and pension pot of in excess of £500k - which you'll access when you actually retire.

If you get all four in harmony, you're sorted.

AT THIS POINT YOU'RE ALMOST OUT OF THERE...

PHASE THREE: THE END-GAME

SAVINGS	HOME	BUSINESS	PENSIONS
TARGET SAVING	EQUITY	EQUITY	TARGET EQUITY
TARGET SAVING	EQUITY	EQUITY	EQUITY
SAVING	EQUITY	EQUITY	EQUITY
SAVING	EQUITY	EQUITY	EQUITY
SAVING	EQUITY	EQUITY	EQUITY
TARGET SAVING	DEBT	TARGET EQUITY	TARGET EQUITY

◀···|······················▶

TAX INEFFICIENT   TAX EFFICIENT

Phase three is for those in their late 40s to early or mid 50s.
Once the end game is achieved - you're completely in the driving seat.
You already have built the pots of wealth up to levels that will take you through to when you want to retire and at the lifestyle that you want to have. (Be realistic here please!)

You'll also need to have planned how you'll exit.

- **Fully** = As I did
- **Arms length** - staying on as a main/minority shareholder, but handing over the day to day to the management team
- **Partially** - Releasing more shares to keep the management team interested. But let them get on with it

YOU'RE ALMOST THERE, TURN THE PAGE TO VIEW THE EXIT

SAVINGS	HOME	BUSINESS	PENSIONS
SAVING	EQUITY		EQUITY
SAVING	EQUITY		EQUITY
SAVING	EQUITY		EQUITY
SAVING	EQUITY		EQUITY

SAVING	EQUITY	EQUITY	EQUITY
TARGET SAVING	DEBT	TARGET EQUITY	TARGET EQUITY

◄ ····································· | ···················· ►

TAX INEFFICIENT   TAX EFFICIENT

112

Phase four is reached when you actually exit. You have all the pots where you want them to be and feel free to do whatever you fancy doing. Carry on working, go cruising, buy a farm!

**Review of the mechanics and the steps you need to take
to execute the plan.**

- Establish what your financial situation is today in each of the four pots
- Do a detailed personal expenditure budget - what does that look like today, next year, five years?
- What does Phase Two/Three look like? How much do you need in each pot at the exit date?
- Ask your accountant about the most efficient ways to get money into the different pots with a view to reducing your personal tax liability
- Involve a **financial advisor in your plan** - find one that has experience in succession planning, exiting businesses and is used to working with entrepreneurs if possible
- Ask your accountant/lawyer if there are tax efficient ways of inviting new shareholders into the business that are accessible and tax efficient for all
- Find a lawyer who has experience in EMI schemes and Management buy-ins
- Prepare a shareholders' agreement that will set out the future and help with any potential conflicts
- Decide on a 'loose' timescale. This should crystallize as time progresses
- Remember as the founder and senior director, it is your business to ensure that the future team is capable of doing what is needed and that they are trained and mentored
- **Hire an experienced advisor, mentor and coach** to help you through this.

In 2017 I exited a business that I founded in 1993. Realistically, for the first 15 years of my agency life I built the business using gut feeling first, business planning second. I even managed to get to revenues in excess of £1m. I was lucky enough to have some fantastic clients and an amazing team.

I then got savvy by spending time with other entrepreneurs and went on a self discovery journey that opened my eyes to the possibility of what could come next. I also went on a course called 'Step Change' delivered by an excellent business coach and author David Hall on behalf of For Entrepreneurs Only. And it was literally a Step Change. It allowed me to think in ways that I'd previously not considered.

Fast forward 10 years or so and I successfully exited the business. It wasn't a life changing amount of money - but it was more than enough to allow me to plan the next decade and third career of my life.

I decided some 10 or so years before the exit what I wanted from the exit and who would be part of the succession plan. I had two excellent department heads, Dom and James and they were prime candidates to take the business over. I really needed them to be part of the team that would take the business further so I offered to sell them 10% each of the business at a reasonable market value (based on Shareholders' funds).

For the next decade we changed the business model, honed our pitch, type of clients and services offered and increased the size of the business in revenue and specialist staff.

In 2016 I was approached by a conglomerate PLC to acquire the business. I took this seriously. But after starting the due diligence I got both cold feet and a feeling that it was against the grain of what I'd agreed with James and Dom back in the day. Once that approach was rejected, I started work with Dom, James, our accountants and legal team to put together a management buy-in that would suit all of us - from a spirit of fairness and willingness to do the deal.

I also brought in another senior member of the team who had vast experience in the Agency sector across Northern agencies and at a senior level. He would help both Dom and James and also be part of the buy in.

By May 2017 I had reduced my working days and in October I left the business but maintained a small shareholding. Whilst I did have a contract with Strawberry to be an at-arms-length consultant I wasn't needed. And I respect that. No one wants the old boss hanging around when the place is under new management!

In November 2017, I started my consultancy business and by March of the next year I had my first client.

My consultancy business has since progressed really well and was only slightly wobbled by the pandemic, thanks to the amazing clients I was working with.

At this time, I took the opportunity to sell the remainder of the shares and finally exited the business I founded some 26 years before. I've often been asked whether this was a sad day. The overall feeling was that the Strawberry Project was over. I'd served my time and new blood had taken it on and would take it in the direction that they saw fit. I was happy. it felt like the end of an era, long live the new era!

When I reflect back to that journey would I have done anything different. Maybe. But not dramatically and it would have been only to probably have started the processes earlier and have certainly employed a consultant/coach like me, as an educated sounding board.

CHOOSING THE SUCCESSION TEAM

Most agency employees like the idea of "making partner", especially if you just hand them free equity. But in reality (for employees and current owners) it tends to be less fun.

QUESTIONS TO ANSWER BEFORE THEY "MAKE PARTNER"

Thinking specifically about your agency, what are your "why" goals behind sharing ownership? Equity partnerships are like a business marriage. Do you truly know the person you're marrying?

Many partnerships start in that form out of necessity. The founders needed to pool their cash. If you're choosing to later create a partnership, you have more flexibility—but also more headaches—to head-off.

"Why?" is the big initial question. Once you dig into why you want to share ownership, consider some more questions about the risks and rewards:

- Would people buy-in via cash, vested sweat equity (EMI scheme), or something else?
- How do you address the value that you—and any other current partners—have built so far, since founding the agency?
- How would you value the business at each buy-in (shareholders' funds)?
- Do key employees have the financial means to buy-in (EMI makes it easier)?
- Do future minority partners have the ability to pay cash taxes each year on their share of the annual profits? Planning and reserving cash for taxes is a good thing
- Do future partners have the ability to infuse cash if something bad happens?
- How much equity would you reserve for yourself?
- As the partnership count increases, is there a point where the financial rewards of an ownership stake become minimal and thus unmotivational?
- What's the personal financial impact to you on a decrease in annual distributions, as you reduce your share from 100% to something smaller?
- What happens if one of your business partners dies, gets divorced, or becomes incapacitated?
- How would you resolve disputes between non-majority partners?

- What would you do if a minority partner wants out, but no one wants to buy their shares at the price they want? In that case, they might receive liquidity—cash—until there's an exit event. And there may never be an exit
- What other restrictive covenants would you include?
- What will you do if a new owner keeps acting like an employee (rather than acting like an owner)?
- What if a partner isn't doing their job? You may be able to fire them as an employee, but depending on the equity terms, they're still an owner; you'd want to create a covenant for this
- What happens when a non-majority owner acts like they're in charge of everything?
- How will you ensure that owners (generally) put the business first?

I'm not saying you shouldn't share ownership; it's good for incentive alignment. But as you can see from the list above, it might be more complicated than it initially seems.

APPENDIX ONE

PROJECT AND RETAINER PRICING THAT WORKS

The trouble with pricing is that there's no right way to do it.
And before you get to the matter of pricing jobs, you need
to realise a few fundamentals of business.

Ultimately what you definitely have to have is a net profit.

In simple terms.

- Revenue less cost of sales = gross profit

- Less your production staff cost (some accountants advise
  that this should go before the gross profit - I don't mind
  as the result is the same)

- Less the directors' costs

- Less central overhead and admin staff cost

- Leaving you with an Earnings Before Interest, Tax, Depreciation
  and Amortisation or EBITDA Profit - which is your trading profit

- Then deduct tax on dividends paid and corporation tax on company
  profits and you have your remaining profit which is then added to
  your shareholders' funds and available for distribution or kept

But to get under the skin of this and understand where you profit
comes from is another matter. The way I prefer to do it is as follows
is to first calculate the sellable value of your production staff.

For example, you have two senior operatives at £50k each, Two middle
operatives at £40k each And Three junior operatives at £25k each
(including National insurance and pension contribution).

They all work 35 hours per week, take 25 holidays, plus 8 bank holidays,
and an average of 5 days sick and the directors chip in with some
billable time as well.

Total Weeks	Hours works per week	Total Hours	Less	Holidays	Bank Holidays	Average Sick Days	
52	35			25	8	5	
		1820		187.5	60	37.5	
Therefore: Total potential hours		1820					
Less holidays / banks / sicks		285					
Total potential hours		**1535**					
					Fixed centre overhead	£60,000	
					Director's cost	£100,000	
Billable time average efficiency		75%			Admin / AC managers	£60,000	
					Therefore central shared overhead is	**£220,000**	
Potential billable hours		1151			Shared between of the earners	£31,429	
					7		
					130%	Profit margin	
				Hourly Cost	Min charge-out rate plus PM		
DIR 1		£55,000		£71	£92	£25,000	
SEN 1		£50,000	£81,429	£71	£92	£105,857	
SEN 2		£50,000	£81,429	£71	£92	£105,857	
MIDD 1		£40,000	£71,429	£62	£81	£92,857	
MIDD 2		£40,000	£71,429	£62	£81	£92,857	
JUNIOR 1		£25,000	£56,429	£49	£64	£73,357	
JUNIOR 2		£25,000	£56,429	£49	£64	£73,357	
JUNIOR 3		£25,000	£56,429	£49	£64	£73,357	
					Potential earnings	**£642,500**	
					Less staff cost	£255,000	40%
					Less Directors	£100,000	16%
					Less Overhead	£60,000	9%
					Less Admin staff	£60,000	9%
					Potential Net profit	**£167,500**	26%

This is a hard one to put your finger on, but you'll probably be somewhere between 65% and 75% efficiency of the time your team is working. You really can't expect more - meetings, briefings, emails, calls, etc. all take time.

Your time recording software will tell you where you are, providing that it's been filled in correctly (that's a totally different story). You should, however, strive for this to be as accurate as possible. The information you get from your systems is very insightful.

How do I use this to calculate my pricing?

You'll see in the chart that a senior should be billed out at £92/hour! If you then times that by 7 hours x £92 x 75% efficiency = £483 that you need to bill them out at per day to make 30% or so margin...

I would never quote an hourly rate. Clients don't factor in efficiency and think that everything should be 100% efficient (which it's definitely not!). They might well divide £483 by 7 and arrive at an hourly rate of £69, which they may perceive to be much better value.

I was working with a client some years ago on a branding project that they needed really quickly. There was a lot riding on it. I quoted £5,000 for the full job. After I left the briefing meeting I had the idea, by the time I'd got back to base I'd developed it and we had the whole pitch and roll-out wrapped up in about 2 days.

I still charged the client £5,000 and they were absolutely delighted! So the key here is clients do not buy your hours, they buy the value you offer them. And this thinking is critical to your success. If you get stuck in a selling hours, you'll never develop very far.

An analogy would be walking into a restaurant and expecting a time calculation against the chef (junior or senior) cooking your dinner - how long did it take them, what was the cost of the ingredients, what overhead contribution was factored in, etc. It's all irrelevant - if you get the dinner you want and the service you expect, you're happy. Similarly, if the client gets what they need at a price they think reasonable, hours are irrelevant. But hours and the cost of those are a starting point and you need to know what your team is costing you and if they're working efficiently.

Referring to Chapter Six, in your business you should have an increasing amount of revenue that I would class as lifetime-value revenue. This is revenue which recurs no matter what. And is in addition to the skills you sell. If you're managing an asset through the technical support contract or providing hosting services these should be extremely profitable. A colleague of mine once referred to this as rent. Imagine having a business that automatically sends out up to 40% of their monthly revenue and expects to have to do little for it, other than manage the process and be there when anything goes wrong – this is lifetime revenue – almost an insurance policy that you're selling.

This revenue goes straight to the bottom line and gets it right and you'll be well on the way to increasing your profitability as you grow.

This makes a scalable business. Most agencies are the opposite; they're growth businesses. Quite often their increased income is not only matched by increased salaries and overheads, it could even outstrip it.

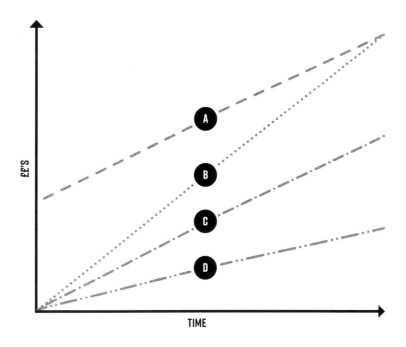

A = Revenue

B = A growth agency will often have an increasing overhead that can, if left unchecked, outstrip revenue, seeing the net profit decrease continuously. This happens more often that you'd think and there have been a few notable agency casualties recently. To the outside world they're growing, getting new clients, expanding territories but under the covers their costs are outstripping their revenues.

C = A growth agency keeps its overhead in line with revenue. In percentage terms the net profit stays the same.

D = The scalable agency gets the golden triangle. They constantly are adding highly profitable lifetime revenue to their business, massively increasing the net profit. This is based on processes and systems rather than headcount.

I once had an interest in a publishing business. They were very successful at selling adverts and getting articles to write, but were terrible at processing them all through to an actual magazine. They built up a huge amount of work-in-progress but got very little revenue going through. Their response was 'to throw bodies at the problem'. This massively increased the cost of doing the business and failed because it just made them even more inefficient.

When I came across this again some years later for another publishing client - they had almost 50 projects (brochures) in production but were only managing to get one out each week.

When I was engaged, I systemised much of the manual work where I could and introduced a proper and easy to follow sign-off process.

We quickly went from producing one a week to two a week and sometimes managed up to four a week. It changed their lives and massively increased their profitability.

This happens in agencies all the time. Their solution to not being able to get the projects out is to either put all of the resources on the one that is nearest the deadline or even worse the one that shouts loudest. This just kicks the can down the road.

APPENDIX TWO

SYSTEMS THAT WORK

I won't go much into this because you more than likely have some in place. However, a little bit of advice is to make sure you're always tuning the systems you have.

7 or so years ago I did a full audit of every system we had running. My list reached 100! A spreadsheet here and there, bits of cloud SAAS, paper (yes paper) it was a tangle. It all worked of course but we'd classically dragged out-moded systems with us over 15 years.

Besides every system I gave a points against its importance, could I get rid or combine could I get it into the cloud (the most important) - I needed the team to be onboard with the change too of course. They have a lot of knowledge so bring them into the discussions.

I managed to reduce to about 25 systems & processes and all in the cloud - and saved a fair bit of money doing it, systems and processes improved and both the team and clients were much happier.

Since then I undertook to do this process every so often.
It's amazing how many 'new' systems pop-up when you're not looking. You just need a regular spring clean and decent tune up.

Systems can also supply you with valuable information on how your agency is performing - covered in the next appendix.

APPENDIX THREE

DASHBOARDS THAT WORKS

KPIs are at the heart of your business. But we can record so much data now that sometimes we just get lost and when we're looking at granular data we sometimes just can't see the wood for the trees.

THIS IS AN IDEAL MONTHLY OPERATIONAL DASHBOARD

- Billable hours available / billable hours chargeable = % efficiency (target 65-75%)
- Revenue invoiced – % of billable hours (above / below target some jobs may be fixed price). If you can do this by client or project, even better
- Less staff, admin and fixed cost, directors cost = net profit for month.
- In addition you should review - your debtors - the money owed to you / overdue
- Cashflow - balance now and anticipated balance (what's your target?)
- What are you focusing on this month to improve?
- Monthly revenue dashboard
- Billing this month - projects, recurring or retained, long term value
- Expected billing next month - 100% confirmed, or 50% confirmed or 10% confirmed
- Expected billing next three months - 100% confirmed, or 50% confirmed or 10% confirmed
- Sales pipeline - long term (the next six months)

MONTHLY CLIENT HAPPINESS DASHBOARD

- Billing this month - projects, recurring or retained, long term value
- Expected billing next month - 100% confirmed, or 50% confirmed or 10% confirmed
- Expected billing next three months - 100% confirmed, or 50% confirmed or 10% confirmed
- Sales pipeline - long term (the next six months)

MONTHLY CLIENT HAPPINESS DASHBOARD

- List each client and get your team to score them out of 10
  (10 being deliriously happy, 1 being about to jump ship). Traffic light
  this and dig into the red zone to ascertain why and what you can do
  to rescue them
- Why are clients in the amber? How can you get them higher
  into the green zone
- Why are clients in the red zone? What are you doing to help?

BUSINESS IMPROVEMENT PROJECTS

- Web-safe
- Digital Production KPIs
- Quality control
- Spring clean of SAAS products

AN IDEAL QUARTERLY DASHBOARD WOULD PAY MORE CLOSE ATTENTION TO PERCENTAGES

- What is the revenue = 100%
- What is the cost of sales = XX%?
- What is the gross profit?
- What is the production staff costs = XX% of gross profit?
  This should be between 40% and 50%. Above this and you're either
  very inefficient or not charging properly
- What is the directors cost = XX% of gross profit?
  Ideally 15-20% and decreasing as the business grows
- What is the admin staff cost XX% of gross profit?
  Ideally no more than 10%
- What is the fixed admin cost XX% of gross profit?
  Ideally no more than 10%
- What is the net profit margin XX% of gross profit?
  Ideally 15-35%

This is a great dashboard to work from - it really is easy to follow
and shows if you're getting better at what you do, more resilient
and layering for the future.

APPENDIX FOUR

THE ROLLING PLAN VS. A FORWARD BUDGET

I'm not a believer in budgets or targets per se.
They're a work of fiction in most cases and can be confusing.
On the whole they don't work in agencies. I prefer a rolling plan.

Yes, the budget elements are fixed costs. These are things
you have some control over.

- Revenue on **projects** is variable
- Revenue on **retainer or regular** clients is 70% secured
- Life-time value revenue is 90% secured

If you work from the three sources of revenue and put this into
a rolling plan then you can project where you may be in 12 months
to 5 years quite easily. Work first with what you know.

You know that half your projects will add revenue to your 2nd stream
(retainer or regular) and you can have an educated guess as to what
revenue that may bring. You also know that projects will end up
delivering the third stream life-time value revenue.

What you can't predict, however, is the amount of revenue that will
arrive as projects - but you can base it on what happened over the last
few years and also what size those projects might be. Grade one might
be a £50k project. Grade two, £20k. Grade three, £10k. Or whatever
your agency is used to.

What you also can't predict is clients disappearing, but if you monitor
the health and happiness of clients you'll have a much better idea.

APPENDIX FIVE

The size of the agency will ultimately depend on how you organise yourselves.

Usually, anything under 5 staff is managed on the fly, with the boss deciding what's going to happen and all others organising the production.

Above that and moving towards a medium sized agency you need to think differently.

You'll probably have different skills teams, such as creative, marketing and development. You may even have dedicated project managers and client account managers.

This is a model that's easy to follow and scale as you need it.

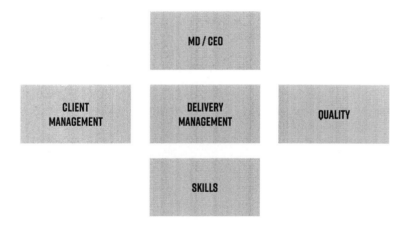

Essentially the client managers are the ones that deal day to day with clients and draw resources from the services teams. This doesn't mean that the client manager is only one who speaks to the client either.

When specialists are needed they get involved but keep the client manager in the loop.

You can keep adding staff to the teams and managers of the clients services as new clients come on board.

The essential point here is that the client manager is the one wholly responsible for the happiness of the client and reports directly to either the MD or the client account director depending on the size of the client.

The delivery management ensures the production and services got delivered as promised. The quality management ensures that the services and products arrive to the quality promised and to the company's values.

I also favour some mirroring. For example, one client services manager would be the main contact but there would always be another who had some knowledge just in case.

The 'skills' people can then be as wide and as varied as the agency needs.

APPENDIX SIX

WHERE WILL YOU WORK FROM?

There have been many articles about where we will all work after the pandemic lockdown is over. Many organisations have already declared that flexible working will be the norm. Others have gone as far to say that they won't have an office or that employees never need to go to the office.

No one argument is right for all, as the circumstances of every organisation is very different, especially with regard to how they deal with their customers.

These are my observations, particularly from a marketing agency perspective.

Working from home suits many but not all and has many obvious benefits to the workforce and the employer.

- It saves commute time
- It allows flexible start and / or finishing times
- It fits around work / life balance
- It attracts those who like this level of flexibility
- It could be that companies can expand, keeping the same office footprint or even reduce it
- It may be that hot desking / laptops become the norm

However, working from home needs routine and discipline, just the same as working in an office and has challenges

- Can you build a team culture remotely? Will employee loyalty suffer?
- Will the homeworker be as effective or efficient?
- How do you measure effectiveness and efficiency even if you wanted to?
- How will you bring on and mentor the younger generation who need more support?
- How do you keep team communications going and relevant?
- How do you support those that are struggling with their mental health or other?
- Everyone will have very different work-from-home circumstances. Some may have a dedicated office, others the kitchen table
- It's even easier to move companies as the location of the employee's home office doesn't move
- What are the H&S implications for home workers?

You now need to weigh up what's right for you and your organisation.

I've started to vision this in bands of team members often based around what they do.

The core management - Operations, account management, quality of output and strategic direction (plus their support team). This is the core team that runs the business and makes it tick. These need to be in the office more often than not as they need to closely interact together.

- **The core management** - Operations, account management, quality of output and strategic direction (plus their support team). This is the core team that runs the business and makes it tick. These need to be in the office more often than not as they need to closely interact together

- **The skill people** - These can be remote or at least use the office from time to time - effectively acting like fully employed contractors. Although I stress there must be extra provision and time given to nurturing the younger members of the team. This has to be formalised and documented

- **The peripheral workers** - Often project based and need little instruction or direction other than ad-hoc or scheduled briefings

If I had my active agency-managing life again and with the modern technologies and SAAS systems available I would have adopted a hybrid system. I would have canvassed all the staff both collectively and individually without pressure or being overly influencing. Once I had found the mood I would have structured it in such a way that everyone knew what their core responsibilities were and where they should / could be based.

I would then ask everyone to stick to a tight routine so that they all knew their roles in the company and expectations.

But, if you want all the team back in the office then I wouldn't disagree either. It's totally up to you what you do - after all it's your business and no decision is wrong providing you've thought it through.